EMANUEL SCHOOL

This book is dedicated to the memory of Lord Hampden,
Chair of Governors 1985–2004.

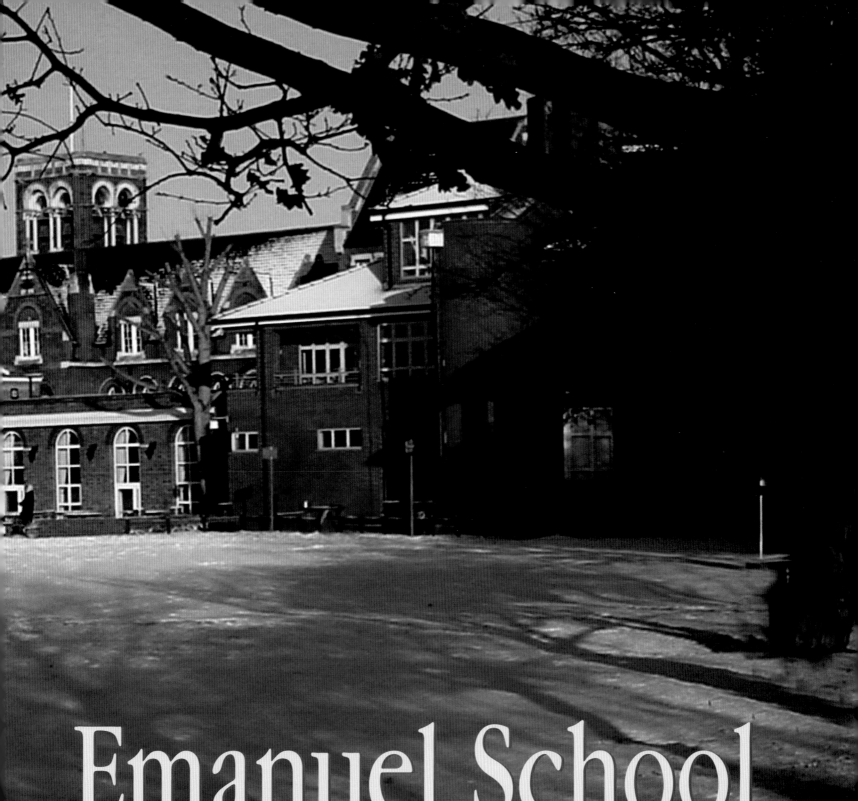

Emanuel School

AN ILLUSTRATED HISTORY

NIGEL WATSON

ISBN 978 1 903942 87 1

First published in 2008
by James & James (Publishers) Ltd
a member of Third Millennium Information
2-5 Benjamin Street
London
EC1M 5QL

www.tmiltd.com

Project Editor and image research: Susan Millership
Design: Vimbai Shire
Production: Bonnie Murray

Photography: John Spragg

Printed in Slovenia by Gorenjski-tisk

Picture Acknowledgements

The bulk of the illustrations come from the School Archive and individual Old Scholars' collections. The Publishers would like to thank all those who have contributed images and in particular, Tony Jones, the School Archivist, for his expert advice and help throughout the project and all the Old Scholars who have contributed material and given generously of their time. The Publishers would also like to thank the following agencies and individuals for permission to reproduce material: National Portrait Gallery 10; Mary Evans Picture Libary 15 (top); © Motco Enterprises Ltd 20; Topfoto 22, 25, 26; The Royal Collection 2006, Her Majesty Queen Elizabeth II 23 (top right); © Hampshire County Council Museums 70, 72 (top left); Petersfield Museum 73 (top), 74 (top), 79 (top); Major Edward Rouse (U.S. Army Retired) 79 (bottom); Roger Clark for many of the pictures in Chapter 6; Aiden Image Portfolio, 150 (Michael Aspel); *The Times* 151 (Simon Barnes);
Le Fevre Communications 150 (Tim Berners-Lee); Tom Phillips 151 (Peter Goddard); James Grant Management 150 (Andi Peters); P Rock 150 (Mick Rock); *Sporting Heroes* 152 (Tom Smith).

Illustrations

Jacket, front: View of Emanuel School.
Back, clockwise from top: Prep First XI; Early photograph of a pupil; Pupils today.
Half title: Monitors, 1889.
Title page: View of the rear of the School on a snowy day.
Page 6: Stained glass window in the chapel.
Page 7: Mark Hanley-Browne, Headmaster 2008.
Page 9: Eagle lectern in the chapel.

Contents

Foreword

EMANUEL IS, HISTORICALLY SPEAKING, one of London's great schools. As any Emanuel student can tell you, we can trace our origins back to 1594 when Lady Dacre made provision in her will for the education of 'ten poore boys and ten poore girls'. Since then many thousands of students have been taught at Emanuel, first in Westminster and then, since 1883, in Wandsworth.

This book has been commissioned to celebrate the past 125 years of Emanuel in Wandsworth, and the main body of this book is about that period. Nevertheless the story would not be complete without a brief look back at the period from 1594 to 1883. So the first chapter relates the story of the Dacre family, the granting of our charter in 1601 by Queen Elizabeth I and how the community was initially presided over by the Warden and Chaplain. Then, in Chapter 2, we are told that a Master was appointed to teach the girls and boys 'reading, writing and creating accounts'. Since then Emanuel has had six Masters and eleven Headmasters, serving between 1736 and 2008, and the school has grown in size from 20 pupils and one Master to over 700 pupils, one Headmaster, 70 teachers and over 40 support staff. The school has also moved from Westminster to Wandsworth, acquired a boathouse in Barnes and bought 14 acres of playing fields at Blagdons near Raynes Park. So the story of Emanuel is a remarkable one, and I wonder if Lady Dacre had any idea, back in 1594, what her little school for 'ten poore boys and ten poore girls' would become over 400 years later!

This is also a story with some dramatic twists and turns. Having been co-educational until 1873, the Governors of the time chose to send the Emanuel girls to other schools in Westminster (mainly to the Grey Coat Hospital School) and so Emanuel in Wandsworth started life as a single-sex boys' school. The school remained 'boys only' until 1995 when girls were finally re-admitted (so please bear this in mind when reading the Appendix of famous OEs!) Another important change was the decision to charge fees for some pupils (pupils prior to 1879 were educated for free). Also the school started life as a boarding school but by 1910 was a school for day boys only. Finally, and perhaps the most dramatic change of all, the school became a voluntary aided grammar school for the period from 1944 until 1976, before reverting back to independence.

The reasons why these changes took place are revealed in this book. However, it is the fact that Emanuel has been through all these changes, and survives to tell the tale, which is the most remarkable thing of all. 'Adapt or die' is one of the basic tenets of evolution theory, and it is because Emanuel has managed to adapt against a backdrop of rapidly changing educational reform that the school is still around in 2008 for Nigel Watson to tell its story.

Mr Watson has written a brilliant book, in my opinion. He has researched it extensively, spending over a year studying our archives and talking to teachers, pupils,

Governors, Old Emanuel pupils and past Headmasters. And that is why I am gratified to read his conclusion that 'the school today . . . is probably more confident in itself and more sure of its own identity than it ever has been'. I hope this is true. Certainly there does seem to be a sense of purpose and a 'buzz' today which, I suspect, has only been matched in the 'Golden Years' of the 1930s and 1950s. I am pleased to report that the pupils today continue to emulate the sporting successes of their predecessors (I came to Emanuel in 2004 and already I have seen five students win international honours in rowing and another three gaining international honours in cricket, football and gymnastics). The current group of artists, musicians and actors are still managing to match, if not exceed, the many achievements of their predecessors. I have also noticed that the students of today are beginning to recapture that sense of scholarship, and the drive for excellence, which seems to have been so prevalent at Emanuel during the 1930s and during the grammar school days. And, without doubt, the competition for places has rarely been as strong as it is today, with around 450 pupils sitting the 11+ exam in 2008 for the 85 places on offer.

But, however popular the school becomes over the next few years, and however spoiled for choice we may be when selecting candidates for entry, I can assure you that we will continue to make offers to students who have a particular talent in music, art, drama or sport, as well as to those who have a particular academic flair. This illustrated history shows that the arts and sport, in particular, have played a key role in buffering us against the waves of change over the

past 125 years. We mustn't let these areas slip back now. We must hold on dearly to our traditions – and, at least while I am Headmaster here, I promise that we will.

Finally, I would like to thank Nigel Watson for the text, Susan Millership for the picture research and her management of this project, Vimbai Shire for the design and all those at James & James who have made this book possible.

Pour Bien Desirer

Mark Hanley-Browne
<small>HEADMASTER</small>
<small>SPRING 2008</small>

Acknowledgements

ALTHOUGH EMANUEL SCHOOL IS an ancient foundation, it has in effect been 'refounded' twice; firstly, in the late 19th century during that period of reforming zeal that transformed so many similar schools and, secondly, since independence in 1976. The current success of the school is a testament to the contribution made to the development of Emanuel by each successive head since 1976. This evolution makes the story of the school particularly fascinating. I have relied on school records, notably magazines and governing body minutes, interviews and the written contributions of many former pupils.

I would like in particular to thank the Head, Mark Hanley-Browne, for his unstinting enthusiasm for the project; his personal assistant, Jill Wood, for helping to provide names, addresses and appointments; Sarah Fisher, the school's development director, for co-ordinating the response from former pupils; Tony Jones, the senior librarian and archivist, for his help, advice and knowledge; the United Westminster Schools Foundation for allowing me access to governing body minutes and other historic material; and the City of Westminster Archives Centre, which stores much of the material relating to Emanuel.

My thanks are also due to all those who have made significant written contributions or given up their time to be interviewed during my research for this book: Lord Hampden, Francis Abbott, Peter Hendry, Peter Thomson, Tristram Jones-Parry, Anne-Marie Sutcliffe, Mary Davies, Tim Hands, Claude Scott, Derek Saunders, Mike Markland, Ray Grainger, Vic Dodds, John Benn, John Hardy, Sara Williams-Ryan, Cliff Lynn, Richard Marriott, Simon Gregory, Ann Thorne, Gary Dibden, Bill Rogers, Paul Hunt, Bill Purkis, Deborah Barty-King, Colin Russell, Rosie Lee, Mary Dobson, Jan Kirkup, John Neale, John Legg, Laura Holmes, Peter Beresford, John Harding, Edgar Asher, Ben Cuddon, Andy Anderson, John Sansbury, Barry Godden, Edwin Page, Henry King, David Davies, Peter Pinkham, John Cheesewright, Dave Nicholson, Tony Layton, Graham Capron-Tee and Jim Cannings.

I hope that within the small canvas of this book I have been able to do some justice to all those who have helped to make it happen.

Nigel Watson
SPRING 2008

Emanuel School traces its history back to 1594 when Lady Anne Dacre left funds in her will to support and educate the poor. Shown here in a painting by Hans Eworth are Lady Dacre's husband, Gregory Fiennes, the tenth Baron Dacre, and his mother.

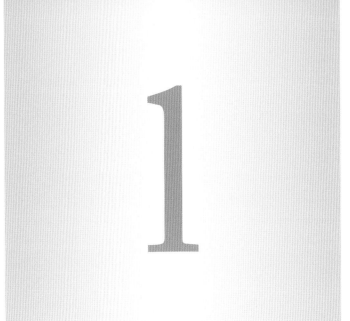

1

1594–1736

The Foundation

'WHEREAS MY LORD IN HIS life tyme and my selfe were purposed to erect an hospital in Westminster or in some other place nere adjoyninge thereunto, and to give one hundred and ten poundes in money towards ye building and edifying thereof and fortie poundes a yere in landes for ever towards ye relife of aged people, and bringing up of children in virtue and good and lawdable artes in ye same hospital, whereby they mighte ye better live in tyme to come by theire honest laboure … To th'end therfor that ye same maye be done accordinglie, with a further augmentacon, I will and devise that myne executors … shall of ye yssues, sales and profits of my mannors, landes and tenements … cause to be erected and builte a meet and convenient house with rooms of habitation for twentie poor folks, and twentie other poor children, employing and bestowing thereupon three hundred poundes …'

And so the will of Anne, Lady Dacre, though she cannot have imagined it, brought into being Emanuel School on 20 December 1594. Her generosity is directly responsible for the school which flourishes today in Wandsworth, south London. With some justification, Emanuel, a fully co-educational school, can also trace back to Lady Dacre the intention to provide equally for girls and boys, while the links with the founder live on through her descendants' continuing involvement. But it was less than clear from her will exactly how she wished children to be brought up in virtue and the good and laudable arts. And from the very beginning her executors were faced with the disadvantage that the endowments left in her will were insufficient. As a result, it was the relief of aged people which claimed first priority for many years while inadequate funds and poor governance combined to delay the opening of the first school until 1736.

Gregory Fiennes, the tenth Baron Dacre, 1590.

By origin, the Dacres come from the village of the same name at the head of Ullswater in Cumbria. During the 13th century the family held important positions in the north. Both William de Dacre and his son Ranulph were Sheriff of Cumberland, Governor of Carlisle Castle and Sheriff of Yorkshire. Ranulph's grandson, another Ranulph, became Baron Dacre of Gilsland in 1321. Four years earlier, through marriage to Margaret de Moulton, he had come into great wealth. She had been betrothed to Ranulph for some time but the death of her father in 1314 threw her marriage into doubt. This made the choice of her husband a matter for her feudal overlord, Edward II, who promised her instead to a seven-year-old boy. But the king was interfering in a love match. In 1317 Margaret eloped with Ranulph from Warwick Castle. Ranulph got away lightly for his disloyalty although he must have been heavily fined. It was certainly enough to keep him faithful to his monarch for the rest of his life. In return, Ranulph too became Sheriff of Cumberland and Governor of Carlisle Castle, leading the English against Scottish raiders, flying his red banner marked with silver escallops, his

retainers wearing the family badge of a red bull, crying 'a Daker, a Daker, a read bull, a read bull'.

In 1458 another woman played a prominent part in the affairs of the family. On the death of the sixth Lord Dacre, Edward IV had to decide whether Dacre's estates should pass to his granddaughter, Joan, daughter of his deceased eldest son, or to his youngest son, Humphrey. Since Edward IV's dubious route to the throne had been secured through the precedence of the senior line by female descent, it was scarcely surprising that the estates passed to Joan. It can only have helped that her husband, Sir Richard Fiennes, was a Yorkist and the King's Chamberlain. Richard's father, Roger, had been a hero at Agincourt and made his home at Herstmonceaux Castle. Richard became Baron Dacre of the South while Humphrey kept the Cumberland estates and took the title of Baron Dacre of the North. Through marriage, Richard's son, John, would inherit the manor of Brandesburton in Yorkshire which later formed part of the endowment made by Lady Dacre.

The family fortunes dipped again in 1541 when the ninth Lord Dacre of the South, Thomas, was executed at Tyburn on 29 June at the age of only 24. A young man who enjoyed a good time, he organised a hunting party for a group of like-minded friends who were staying with him at Herstmonceaux. Unfortunately the deer they chased belonged to Thomas's neighbour, Sir Nicholas Pelham, and in the fracas which ensued between the hunters and Sir Nicholas's servants, one of the latter was fatally wounded. The evidence was inconclusive as to whether Thomas was personally responsible and, if he was, it seems likely he was acting in self-defence. He entered a

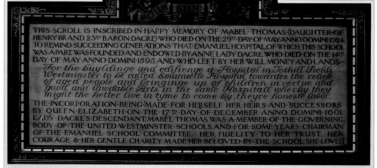
The Mabel Thomas Memorial commemorating Lady Dacre's foundation of the school hangs in the library.

Stained glass in the chapel showing the Dacre family crest.

last of the Fiennes to be Baron Dacre. The death of their son may have been one reason for founding Emanuel Hospital, on which work began around the time of Geoffrey's death in September 1594. But family tradition also has it that Lady Dacre resented that the bulk of the family estates would pass to her sister-in-law and decided out of spite that any free land should be placed beyond her sister-in-law's reach.

The three to four acre site in Westminster was bounded by the present day Palace Street, Buckingham Gate and Castle Lane. The name was stipulated by Lady Dacre. Emanuel (more usually, Emmanuel) means God With Us and the foundation was clearly intended to have a religious, and Protestant, nature. But no provision was made for a resident chaplain and instead the incumbent of St Margaret's, Westminster, was paid a small retainer to visit the Hospital. In Tudor times this indicated only an institution where the poor and elderly were cared for, the sick were visited and religious instruction provided. The religious character of the Hospital inherited by the school remains important at Emanuel today.

plea of not guilty and would probably have been acquitted or escaped with a fine. Instead, for whatever reason, he withdrew his plea and threw himself on the king's mercy. Henry VIII was the wrong king to choose. Persuaded by Thomas's enemies of his guilt, he sentenced the young nobleman to death.

But the king never sequestrated the family estates. Seventeen years later Geoffrey, Thomas's second son, and Margaret, his daughter, paid a hefty fine to clear the family's name and retrieve their estates by Act of Parliament. Geoffrey was not a strong man, molly-coddled and dominated by his mother, contemporary records describing him as 'a little crack-brain'd'. But the return of his estates made him an eligible bachelor. Sir Richard Sackville, Treasurer of the Exchequer, nicknamed 'Fill-Sack' for obvious reasons, seized the chance to marry off his daughter Anne to Geoffrey. It was Anne who would endow Emanuel.

Anne's father was related to Anne Boleyn and through this connection she became a maid of honour to Queen Elizabeth. Anne inherited her father's strength of character and, given her husband's weakness of mind, took over the running of the family estates. But the couple's only son died an infant, leaving Geoffrey as the

The Sackville family crest in the chapel. Lady Anne Dacre was a Sackville before marrying Baron Dacre.

Lady Dacre died on 14 May 1595 and lies alongside her husband in Chelsea Church. Her will increased her husband's benefaction and also assigned the manor of Brandesburton and its rental income to the Hospital. The buildings, brick with tiled roofs, provided two rows of ten rooms each, with the chapel and other offices erected along a third side. A charter of incorporation was granted on 17 December 1601. At the same time, the executors of Lady Dacre's will, Sir Drue Drury, Constable of the Tower of London, Edward Fenner, Edward More and George Gorringe, drew up statutes for the Hospital. They became the first governors of Emanuel and, most importantly for future developments, directed through the statutes that the beneficiaries of the will should be drawn from the parishes in which the Dacres had property, namely, Westminster, Chelsea and Hayes. After the death of the last of the original governors, Sir Edward More, in 1623, the responsibility for the management of the Hospital passed to the Lord Mayor and Aldermen of the City of London.

The first indication that the executors-cum-governors were trying to implement Lady Dacre's wishes for the upbringing of 20 poor children came in the Hospital statutes of 1601. These permitted each of the 20 poor residents to keep and bring up one poor child 'in some good and laudable art, or science, wherby hee or shee may be better in tyme to come lyve by their honest labor'. Apprenticeship, rather than education, seemed to be the intention. This would have been in tune with the times, for formal education was restricted almost entirely to the grammar schools, which taught boys only, and, from the early 17th century onwards, to a handful of private schools which educated girls. But the provision in the statutes was obviously made more in hope than expectation since it seems highly unlikely that any of the Hospital's residents would have had either the money or the inclination to take in a child.

The first governors took more of an interest in the Hospital than their successors. Certainly it was a small charity, but the Corporation of the City of London governed it through neglect, paying little attention to the statutes. It was more than 40 years before anyone took any notice and decided in 1669 that an investigation ought to be held. Another four years passed before a

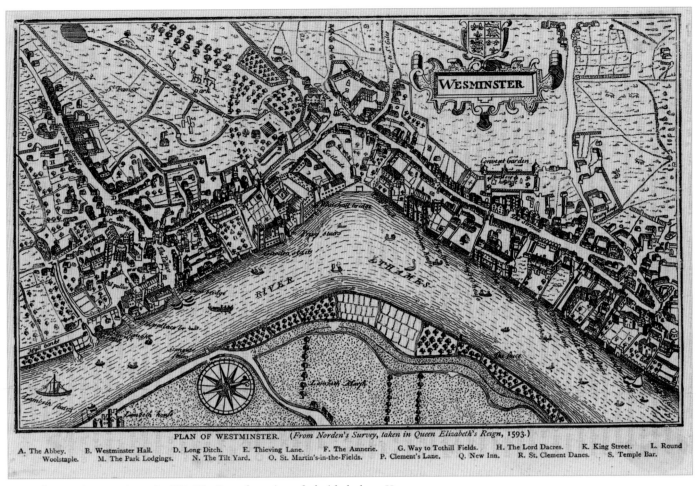

PLAN OF WESTMINSTER. *(From Norden's Survey, taken in Queen Elizabeth's Reign, 1593.)*

A. The Abbey. B. Westminster Hall. D. Long Ditch. E. Thieving Lane. F. The Amnerie. G. Way to Tothill Fields. H. The Lord Dacres. K. King Street. L. Round Woolstaple. M. The Park Lodgings. N. The Tilt Yard. O. St. Martin's-in-the-Fields. P. Clement's Lane. Q. New Inn. R. St. Clement Danes. S. Temple Bar.

Map of Westminster, as it was in 1593. The Dacre house is marked with the letter H.

report was issued which encouraged the Aldermen to start visiting the Hospital twice a year. It was a further nine years before the statutes were revised to prevent any more irregularities. Such neglect was not an isolated example. Future governors 250 years later would be criticised in much the same way.

The 1682 statutes spelled out for the first time the intention of the Hospital governors to admit children as soon as revenues permitted. More than that, the governors also intended to build accommodation for them and employ a master and a mistress to teach and look after them. But they had to wait until the existing one hundred year lease of the Brandesburton estate expired in 1695. With the new lease increasing the annual rent from £100 to £360, they

could begin accumulating the funds they needed. With the increased rent the governors were able to build new almshouses in 1701, rebuild the chapel in 1728 and finally erect accommodation to house a master and children.

In 1732 a committee of Aldermen finally recommended that the time had come to admit children to the Hospital in accordance with Lady Dacre's will. It was clear that the residents had never been capable of giving instruction to children. Contemporary accounts show that some pensioners were utterly unsuitable to care for children. In 1735, for instance, the Hospital Warden, William Butt, reported the disgraceful behaviour of some of his charges. He had 'read over divers times the Written Rules of this Hospital to the Pensioners, notwithstanding which they have no regard to them, but return abusive language, more particularly Mrs Norcott, who has for a constancy [friend] a very evil tongued Woman that is with her Night and Day, and grossly uses him [the Warden] to the incouragement of all the rest'. The Hospital also seems to have been a target of local vandals. The Warden complained about 'a number of idle disorderly Boys that plays before the Gates of the Hospital in a very disturbing manner, to the great indangering of the Hospital's being set on Fire by frequent throwing in of Squibs, especially into the first House of the Women side'.

The governors decided that a married clergyman should be found to teach the children they proposed to admit to the Hospital. His duties would also include taking chapel for the residents, perhaps in the hope that a resident chaplain would have a greater influence upon their conduct. While the governors expected each of the 20 children to have their clothing provided by family or friends, a sum of £12 a year was allocated to each one to cover the cost of teaching them, feeding them, keeping them clean and providing them with bedding. The boys were to learn reading, writing and accounts, and the girls would be taught to read, write and 'work plain work', some form of simple sewing. No child younger than seven would be taken nor any child older than 15. They would be drawn from the parishes of Westminster (17), Chelsea (2) and Hayes (1).

FACING PAGE, LEFT: *The chapel at the heart of Emanuel Hospital, showing the eagle lectern, altar and pulpit that were moved to the school's present chapel in the 19th century.* ABOVE: *The newly refurbished chapel at Emanuel School, Wandsworth, 2007.*

2

1736–1883
The First School

In 1736, ALMOST 150 YEARS AFTER Lady Dacre's death, the first school under her endowment opened its doors to welcome 20 specially selected poor children, ten boys and ten girls. In charge of them was the first Master, an Anglican clergyman called Thomas Bolton. From the brown serge uniform worn by successive generations of children until 1869, the school became known as the Browncoat School.

School hours were long and holidays short. The day began at six in the morning, with a two-hour break from eleven until one, finishing at five o'clock. In winter the day started an hour later. In 1795 the timetable was changed by cutting an hour from each session during summer and two during winter. Holidays totalled ten days, taken at Easter, Whitsuntide, Bartholomewtide and Christmas. Judging from a surviving 1784 diet sheet, the children were well fed. They had plenty of meat, vegetables, bread and cheese, with small beer to wash it all down. Small beer was very weak ale, a much healthier option than drinking untreated water. So, for instance, the children had boiled beef, with greens, turnip and broth, for lunch on Thursdays, while breakfast was always bread and small beer, and supper bread with either butter or

Painting of Emanuel Hospital in Westminster, as it looked in the mid-nineteenth century. The Warden is carrying the school's ceremonial mace.

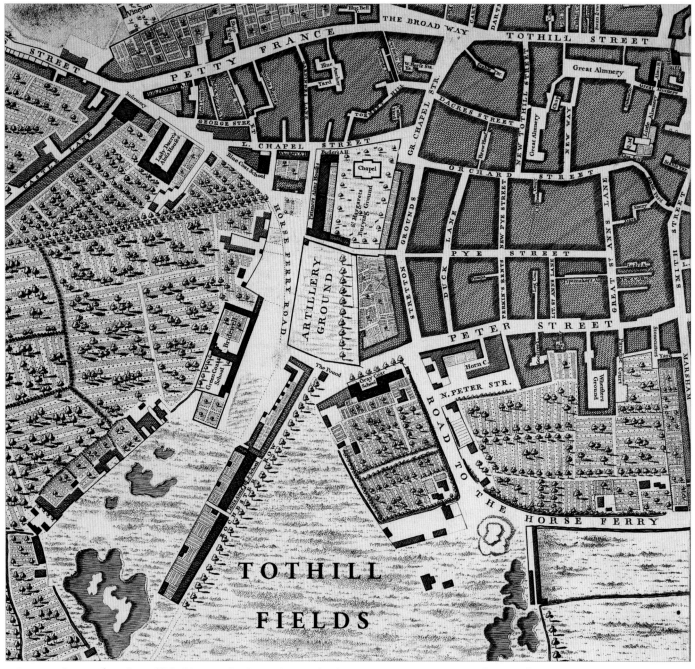

John Rocque's map of London published in 1746 showing Lady Dacre's Alms Houses in Westminster, the first site of the school.

cheese. The elementary education covered reading, writing and arithmetic, with the girls taking needlework rather than arithmetic. English grammar and the catechism were added to the curriculum in the early 19th century. All the children took their turn in cleaning the chapel, one boy rang the bell for prayers, the boys worked in the garden and the girls helped in the laundry and kitchen. In later years the girls also made and mended linen for the Hospital. The children were placed in employment when they left school. Between 1796 and 1804, for instance, boys were apprenticed as shoemakers, bookbinders, wheelwrights, turners, masons and watch finishers, with one working for a mail coach manufacturer. Girls found places with mantua makers (a mantua was a loose gown worn over a petticoat), tailors, bowstring makers and a manufacturer of silk stockings.

The milk of human kindness seems to have been largely absent from Thomas Bolton. He was a barbarous, bad-tempered and ill-natured man. The school had not been open long when he allowed two of the older girls to take the cane to a younger girl who had misbehaved. She was so badly treated that her father came to the school to protest. The unfortunate parent refused to leave until Bolton, who painted as black a picture of him as possible in making his report to the governors, had beaten him up. But complaints from parents about the ill-treatment of their children at Bolton's hands kept rolling in. In 1737 their allegations ranged from confinement without food or drink for several hours to giving them water instead of small beer. There was probably some truth in these but it turned out that many of the complainants had been bribed. They had been liberally plied with gin by the Warden of the Hospital, jealous of the Master's superior position, and a member of staff sacked by Bolton. The Master complained to the governors that he had been sent anonymous letters, calling him a son of a bitch, his wife a stinking carrion and his maid a nasty blackguard bitch. He was cleared, the rules were tightened up and both sides were told to watch their future behaviour.

Bolton seems to have lasted until 1742 and his 18th-century successors led much less scandalous lives. The number of children in the school remained constant for the rest of the century, although between 1795 and 1802 eight boys were taught in a small school at Brandesburton, the foundation's Yorkshire property, where costs were much lower. This ceased in 1802 when the governors concluded it was outside their remit but they built a school on land they owned in Brandesburton in 1843. In 1821 it was agreed to double the numbers of pupils but although the extra buildings that were needed were completed in 1824, it was another 20

A boy in the brown serge uniform of Emanuel Hospital, 1842.

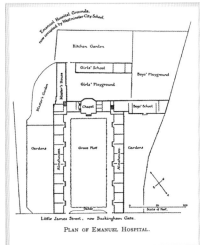

Plan of Emanuel Hospital in the 1850s showing the separate boys' and girls' schools behind the chapel.

years before the additional boys and girls were admitted. The way in which the increase was implemented would prove controversial since the governors did not allow Westminster the same proportion of places, giving them just over half, with the bulk of the rest drawn from the City. From that time until 1873 a handful of boys from Brandesburton also found their way into the school. The age range was changed as well, with pupils admitted between the ages of seven and nine and leaving at 14. It was probably around this time that the sexes began to be taught separately from each other, then common practice.

The Master during this period was Dr R J Waters, the longest-serving of them all, in office from 1804 until 1858. Waters seems to have led a happy ship, marred by the occasional tempest. The worst came at the very end of Waters' time when he appointed to the staff a former pupil called John Causier. He turned out to be a schoolmaster of the brutal kind, wielding the cane only too freely. This provoked uproar among the pupils, leading, reported Waters, to a 'state of anarchy and misrule', and the absconding from the school of several boys with previously unblemished records. But Waters himself brought a civilizing influence to the school. By the middle of the century, he had added history, geography, algebra, French and singing to the curriculum. He was in effect running a small boarding school. Emanuel was never burdened by the failings of the endowed grammar schools, whose sorry decline, stemming in part from their narrow and unreformed curriculum, would provoke the educational upheaval which caught Emanuel in its net later in the century. Neither was Emanuel part of the wave of new public schools, most famously illustrated by Dr Arnold's Rugby in *Tom Brown's Schooldays*. It was an

School trips. BELOW: *The school visited the Great Exhibition at Crystal Palace, 1851.*

FACING PAGE: *On a trip to the Zoo in Regent's Park in 1850 the pupils would have seen Obaysch, the first hippopotamus in Britain. His arrival was a sensation, attracting up to 10,000 visitors a day, spawning hippo memorabilia and even a dance – the Hippopotamus Polka.*

unusual creation, and ploughed its own middle course under the distant governance of the Corporation of the City of London.

Although the daily routine changed little, holidays were extended, giving a week at Christmas plus a month in midsummer. The boys from Yorkshire were given extra time in summer since it was impossible for them to return home at Christmas. School food appeared to be a monotony of mutton, mainly boiled, to the extent that on one occasion in 1857 all except two of the children refused to eat it. Instead, it was served up to them the following day when they ate it voraciously. But by all accounts the pupils were remarkably healthy, seeming to escape the many potentially fatal ailments of the age. They also enjoyed occasional days out, for Waters was ahead of his time in introducing the sort of excursions for his pupils which for some schools were innovative even in the 1920s. In July 1850 they spent a day at the zoo in Regent's Park, followed in June 1851 by an outing to the Great Exhibition, attracting favourable comments for their appearance and behaviour. A walk in Kensington Gardens in April 1859 did not quite go to plan. It was reported that one boy, Davies, 'had run out of the Gardens into Kensington and come back unwell. He confesses to have gone into a public house and drunk a

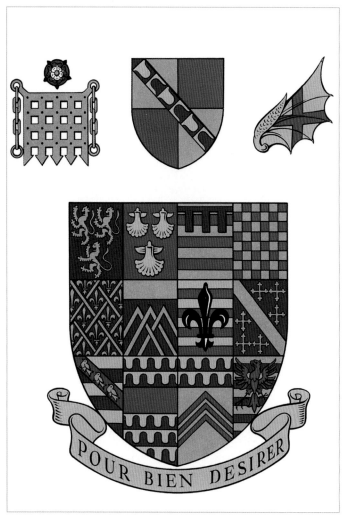

The Emanuel School arms combine the shields and mottos of the Dacre and Sackville families. The Rose and Portcullis denote the school's early connection to Westminster and the silver dragon's wing with the red cross represents the crest of the City of London.

pint of porter'. But such visits were treats and, as one former pupil wrote, 'we saw little of the outside world; our lives were of a cloistered kind, but we were on the whole quite a happy and contented crowd of hearty, healthy boys ... we were certainly given a fair start in the worldly race'.

Waters must have been much missed by those pupils who remained at the school under his successor, Arthur Mozley, another clergyman, in charge until 1869. He ran a regime at once severe yet prone to indiscipline. One girl admitted at the age of eight had all her warm clothing taken from her and was expected to carry out a wide range of domestic duties, from cleaning and dusting to washing and ironing, acting as housemaid to the

chaplain. Again there were complaints from parents and again to no avail. Yet the girl in question was truly grateful for the education she received, later recalling that 'we only had a very elementary education but we learned a good many things that girls do not learn nowadays, and although it was a drastic training it has been very useful and has helped me through life'.

The incident which precipitated Mozley's departure was an act of mass disobedience by the boys in 1869 when, among other things, they refused to work in the garden or to eat their meals. The governors investigated and were very critical of the Master's poor management of the school and his neglect of the statutes for the sake of an easy life. For Mozley, this was the pot calling the kettle black, and he noted sharply in his response that 'I should have been glad if more of the Governors had made themselves personally acquainted with the work of the place'. The same girl who had talked of her 'drastic training' also remembered how 'a few of the Aldermen used to come at times and look at us, and one we disliked so much because he always objected to our having anything different in the way of clothing; he said we were quite saucy enough as it was'.

By the time Mozley left in 1869, English education was on the cusp of reform. There was a feeling that England was being left behind by other nations. It is calculated that only between two-thirds and three-quarters of school-age children were at some sort of school by 1870. At the same time the 1867 Reform Act had made sweeping changes to the voting system, creating almost unlimited household suffrage in the country's urban seats, bringing in a swathe of new voters and leaving one conservative politician to ask what was left 'to save the Constitution from the hands of a multitude struggling with want and discontent'. There was a widespread feeling that the state should take a more direct role in the provision of education. For those on the right, education seemed to be a defence for the constitution; for those on the left, it was the key to advancement.

The first change came with W E Forster's great Education Act of 1870. To achieve a political and religious consensus, it was limited in scope. But for the first time every child had the chance of an elementary education. Fees were paid by all but the poorest until 1891 but it was the poorest the Act sought to catch. School attendance was not made compulsory until 1880 but there was little point in compulsion until schools had been built and teachers trained. The minimum school leaving age was raised from 10 to 11 in 1893 and again to 12 in 1899, the only exception being children involved in agriculture. All this was an enormous step forward. Success in conquering mass illiteracy was evident in the 1886 general election when fewer than 39,000 out of 2.4 million votes were cast by men unable to read or write.

The provision of state elementary education inevitably changed the position of schools like Emanuel, even though its curriculum was rather more advanced than many of the new state-sponsored schools. But Emanuel's position was already under review by 1870 as the simultaneous reform of secondary education swept through charitable schools across the country. The 1867 report of the Taunton Commission had identified a great national need for secondary schools, blaming this largely on the failings of the grammar schools. The Commission's solution was to utilize the charitable endowments devoted mainly to the grammar schools but also to schools like Emanuel to create a system of secondary schools catering largely for the middle classes. The Endowed Schools Commission was established with the power to revise the statutes of the endowed schools, to appropriate parish charities for education and to oversee any subsequent educational schemes. The Commission and its staff set to work with gusto, without fear of treading on the toes of vested interests, making as many enemies as friends. Its life was short but effective and in any case its replacement, the Charity Commission, formed in 1874, exercised much the same powers in much the same way.

Of all the schools reformed by the Endowed Schools Commission, the most politically challenging was Emanuel. The governors, perhaps more sensitive to the political trends of the day, could see the pattern emerging nationally through the work of the Commission. They had read the Taunton Commission's adverse remarks, that the pupils admitted to the school were unfit to benefit from the education being provided, even though it was of an elementary nature; that they were selected in an ad hoc manner on the whim of the governors who had

their particular favourites; and that they were no longer drawn from the ranks of the poor but from the families of those who worked as messengers in Parliament or were employed by the governors. The report concluded that 'these endowments now act largely, though indirectly, in the discouragement of education, and they are applied very frequently to the relief of classes of persons who could hardly have been regarded by the Founders as within the immediate purview of their intentions'.

The governors therefore seized on the appointment in 1869 of Mozley's successor, the Reverend Maskell, as the perfect opportunity to devise their own scheme of reform. They considered they could abolish the almshouses, providing pensions instead for the elderly poor, and relocate the school to some rural location in the home counties, where they would pay to educate and clothe 70 boys and girls, admitting others on the payment of fees. The Commission's scheme followed in 1870. This saw no independent future for Emanuel Hospital. Instead it proposed uniting the endowments of four local charities covering Emanuel, St Margaret's Hospital, established in 1633, Palmer's School, founded in 1650, and Hill's Grammar School, founded in 1708, under one

Punch cartoon showing William Edward Forster, the architect of the Education Act of 1870, telling children that they are entitled to a basic education despite the wrangling of the politicians and churchmen shown in the background.

THE THREE R's; OR, BETTER LATE THAN NEVER.

governing body to provide a boarding school for 300 boys and another for 120 girls, with two new Westminster day schools, each for 300 boys, and the maintenance of the Grey Coat school for girls. Endowments currently serving 230 children would provide a secondary education for 1,320.

The battle lines were drawn. The Commission was faced with an adversary in the Lord Mayor and Aldermen of the City of London far more powerful than any it had faced before. The arguments passionately debated over the next three years focused on three main principles: admission by patronage or competitive entrance examinations; the educational needs of the poor against those of the better off; and self-regulation rather than state interference. The battle was fought through petitions presented to the government, protest meetings held at the Mansion House, the letters column of *The Times* and ultimately in Parliament itself. Maskell defended the selection of pupils for the school, 'the destitute children of the lower middle class', 'the children of decayed and distressed householders', a class of society which, he wrote, 'would be simply rendered helpless and driven into pauperism but for the help of institutions like Emanuel Hospital'. In the House of Lords, the case for Emanuel was put by Lord Salisbury, later prime minister, who warned of the dangers of confiscating the inheritance of the poor; while Lord Halifax took the opposite view, condemning the education of so few children on an annual income of £4,000 (£2.5 million today). When the debate opened in Parliament, Emanuel became a national *cause célèbre*, the arguments for and against featuring in the editorials of leading newspapers and magazines.

The Lords threw out the Commission's scheme but the Commissioners simply drew up a new scheme less vulnerable to attack. This time they left the administration of the almshouses in the hands of the Corporation while providing more than

Prime Minister William Gladstone dramatically altered the course of history for Emanuel with his speech to the House of Commons in 1871.

half the places on the new united governing body for representatives of the Lord Mayor and Aldermen. A boys' boarding school, called Emanuel School, would be established within 20 miles of London while two day schools for boys would be created in Westminster (ultimately they were merged into the Westminster City School in 1899). To counter criticism that the Commission was stealing the inheritance of the poor, the scheme created a large number of places (foundationers) exempt from fees and available to poor boys in adversity. To make the school more accessible to a wide section of society, a limit was also set on fees. A separate scheme was devised – and passed without argument – for the Grey Coat School.

On 13 May 1873 the new scheme governing Emanuel came before the House of Commons. Immediately moved for rejection, it was Gladstone's intervention, in a long, sharp, often witty and outstanding speech, which ensured that the motion was crushed and the scheme accepted. He asked why the only scheme drawn up by the Commission which had ever caused any contention related to Emanuel and he criticized the scheme's opponents for demanding that 'there shall be one law for the world at large and another for the Corporation of London'. To accept that, he suggested, would be 'to check the progress of practical reform'. He pointed out that, while the City was eager to hang on to the financial benefits of the Hospital, Lady Dacre's will clearly intended that the principal beneficiaries should be chosen from the parishes of Westminster, Chelsea and Hayes, which the governors had ignored whenever the number of pupils had been increased. Gladstone was scathing in his comments on the actions of the Corporation in 1844. He said:

'Their thought was how much they could draw into the City of London – a city fed with charities, gorged and almost bloated with charities, that remarkable city containing a larger extent of property

The Emanuel Mace dates from 1845.
The Dacre arms are engraved on one
side and those of the City of London
on the other. On the top is a woman
(intended to be Lady Dacre) carrying
a child with two children beside her.

This and facing page: *The fine 17th-century paintings of Moses* (ABOVE) *and Aaron* (OPPOSITE) *which hang on either side of the chapel doors were bought by the governors in 1673.*

devoted to so-called public objects, and for the application of which it is impossible to give satisfactory reason, than any other city in the country. Though Westminster was poor to the lowest depths of poverty, and London was rich up to almost a splendid magnificence of wealth, that Committee [of the Corporation] looked into the deed, and reported that, as they were advised, there was nothing in it to prevent their admitting other parishes to the benefits of the foundation, and notably the people of London.'

When the vote was taken, the supporters of the scheme triumphed by 286 votes to 238.

It was another decade before the re-founded Emanuel School emerged. By then girls had left the school. Under the scheme, a separate foundation was established to look after girls' education while the four charities, including Emanuel, were placed under one governing body, the United Westminster Schools Foundation (UWF). Most of the girls transferred to the Grey Coat School in 1873 while the Grey Coat boys, plus boys from St Margaret's Hospital, moved to Emanuel. Maskell was marking time at the Hospital and, while he added Greek and Latin, chemistry and physics to the timetable, the regime remained spartan. One former pupil from the 1870s recalled that 'we were not allowed outside the school walls, and had no contact with the world beyond the gates or with other schools'. Pupils were not allowed to read novels and games were limited to indoor activities, such as chess and draughts. In 1878 the incident known as 'The Great Rebellion' took place when senior boys stole provisions and took possession of the dormitory, holding out for the next day and night, giving in on the second day, after negotiations conducted through dormitory windows with masters clinging on to the tops of ladders. The ringleaders were expelled and the remainder told not to return after the holidays. One outcome appears to have been the introduction of organized outdoor games to keep the boys occupied and run off their energy.

In 1879, when the roll stood at 51, the last of the boys belonging to the old Hospital foundation left the school. Of the new intake, 21 were nominated from local elementary schools, 22 were admitted on the grounds of adversity or as orphans, seven were paying half-fees and only one full fees. Some of these boys, noted Maskell, were 'not much better than "street boys" in general behaviour'. With closure looming, there was a reluctance to spend money on either the buildings or teaching materials. He lamented that 'under these circumstances many subjects are taught here with but partial success, because of the difficulties of the place. French, for instance, by English teachers; Latin to many boys who leave us before they can finish the Grammar; Chemistry with only a few materials the property of the Master and other Branches of Science without diagrams or adequate modern apparatus.'

On 17 December 1882 the old school finally closed its doors. The Hospital was demolished in 1894 to make way for the block of apartments known as St James's Court. The new school was given the furniture from the Hospital chapel, the altar table, eagle lectern, oak pulpit and sanctuary chairs, which themselves had originally come from the demolished church of St Benetfink in Cheapside. With them also came the two paintings of Moses and Aaron which had been purchased in 1673 for £12.

In the meantime, preparations were being made to open the new school. The UWF clearly intended the new boys' boarding school should be in the countryside and a site was bought at Swanley in Kent in 1879. It was not good timing. With rural England in the grip of an agricultural depression, land values and rental income were falling so the income of the Foundation, gained primarily from the Brandesburton estates, was no longer sufficient to build a new school. This was the first of a series of compromises forced upon the school by inadequate endowments. The idea was abandoned, the Swanley site sold and, under increasing pressure to produce results, the governors bought an existing property in Wandsworth for £32,000 in March 1882. There was still an open feel to the borough in the early 1880s, for the encroachment of suburbia was some years off. The premises acquired by

The oak pulpit in the chapel.

the Foundation had been built scarcely a decade earlier as the Royal Patriotic Asylum for Boys. The Asylum was actually an orphanage for the sons of those servicemen who had lost their lives during the Crimean War (a similar institution, on land close by, was also built for girls). It quickly ran out of money as well as orphans and the buildings were put up for sale. Imposing, designed in a classical style, they were constructed in red brick, and located on 12 acres in what was almost open countryside, adjacent to Wandsworth Common and sandwiched between two railway lines. The only problem was that the Foundation was in a hurry to get the new school up and

FACING PAGE: *The east window in the chapel. The central panel is dedicated to Arthur Towsey, the first Headmaster and chaplain of Emanuel School when it moved to Wandsworth.* ABOVE: *The earliest known photograph of Emanuel pupils and a master, 1885.*

running and not a great deal of thought was given to re-planning the buildings for use as a school. In any case, funds had been all but exhausted by the purchase and little was left for fitting out the buildings. As a consequence, improvements were made in an unsatisfactory and piecemeal fashion over the years.

The Foundation had other things to attend to. There was a Headmaster to appoint. One hundred applications were received which the governors reduced to two candidates, the Reverend C Butler and the Reverend A Towsey. In July 1882, after

The Reverend A Towsey, Headmaster, 1883–93.

interview, they both claimed five votes each. Only the chairman's casting vote made Arthur Towsey the first Headmaster – and chaplain – of Emanuel School in Wandsworth. Born in 1851, educated at the City of London School alongside Herbert Asquith, he went up to St John's, Cambridge, at the age of 17. The loss of an eye at the end of his first university term was an omen of the ill-health he would suffer throughout the rest of his life. On 22 January 1883 he welcomed the first 80 boys, 68 boarders and 12 day boys, to the first day of the first term of the new school.

Flannels Day, 1912.

1883–1919
Beginnings in Wandsworth

W ITH A PROUD TRADITION and buildings with great potential, Emanuel School seemed to have a lot going for it. Establishing the school in Wandsworth, however, proved to be a difficult task. Towsey and his successors, Arthur Chilton, Henry Buchanan Ryley and Shirley Goodwin, had to overcome the challenges of unsatisfactorily adapted buildings and poorly paid staff.

Towsey quickly discovered that the teaching accommodation was poor. His initial request for an additional classroom was turned down by the governors although gradually they did sanction a variety of works and improvements. The pressure to improve the buildings increased with the number of boys. In the summer of 1883, there were 117 boys, including 27 day boys, at the school. Six years later, there were 270, of whom 85 were day boys. After a chemistry laboratory was built in 1885 nothing more was done until 1895, when three new classrooms, more laboratories, a lecture room, art room and hall were constructed. In 1902, when less than half of the 340 boys were boarders, music rooms were built, and in 1905 the metal workshop was

The altar table in the chapel.

completed and one of the dormitories was divided into two classrooms. The possibility of installing electric lighting was raised in 1903 but took 30 years to materialize. More laboratories and classrooms were added in 1910, by which time there were 500 boys. Since boarding had almost vanished, the old sanatorium was used to start a junior school. The inspectors, who first visited the school in 1906 and then again in 1910, politely raised the need on both occasions for further improvements.

Boarding turned out to be short-lived. The number of boarders peaked at 185 in 1889 and fell steadily thereafter, reaching 110 in 1907. Unsatisfactory living conditions may have been one reason but the main cause was the steady urbanization of the local area. It made boarding pointless. Parents who wanted

Plaque marking the school's move to Wandsworth in 1883.

their sons to board sent them to schools in truly rural surroundings beyond the city and its suburbs. Emanuel was faced with having to redefine its role as a day school.

This would not be easy. Little thought had been given to the school's catchment area when the school premises were purchased. Scholarships were given to boys taken from the parishes traditionally associated with the charity but the increasing number of London day schools made it seem unlikely that Emanuel could count on them in the future. It would have to establish itself as the local day school of choice.

Although it was increasingly obvious that if Emanuel had a future, it was as a day school, serious consideration was given in 1908 to transferring the whole school to another boarding school in Kent. This was the William Lambe Grammar School at Sutton Valence, originally run by the

School nurse.

Clothworkers' Company but transferred in that year to the UWF. The governors considered inviting London County Council to take over the Wandsworth premises. More sensibly, it was decided to transfer the remaining Emanuel boarders to Kent but to develop Emanuel as a day school, given the rising demand for day school places within London. The decision to close down the boarding side of the school was made on 29 March 1909 and by the end of the year dormitories were being converted into classrooms. The few remaining boarders were moved to an approved boarding house run by 'Ma' Sisterson in nearby Spencer Park. All of them had left the school by 1913. The governors hoped to increase the school roll to at least 750. It would be a struggle. On the eve of the First World War, numbers were still less than 600.

Emanuel quickly became the middle-class secondary school that the Endowed Schools Commission had always intended. In 1906 when there were already more day boys (231) than boarders (128), pupils were drawn overwhelmingly from the ranks of the middle class, although their backgrounds ranged from the professions and merchant banking to shop owners and clerks. Only 24 boys came from the homes of artisans, that is, the skilled working class. With almost 200 coming from Wandsworth itself, it initially seemed as if the school was proving attractive to local middle-class parents after all. Moreover, as boarders disappeared, the school succeeded in replacing them with boys from other parts of London. So, when the inspectors next turned up in 1910, fewer (147) of the 525 boys on the roll came from Wandsworth while the rest were drawn from elsewhere in the capital. Another important development which helped the school to adjust was the rising intake of London County Council (LCC) scholars, sent to the school from various local-authority elementary schools. They formed more than one-third of pupils in 1910. Since the usual proportion accepted by schools under the Board of Education Regulations in return for LCC funding was 25 per cent, this suggests that Emanuel was not actually benefiting from the growing demand for day-school places and was instead having to take in more scholars to keep the school reasonably full. The fact that very few of the candidates taking the school's entrance examination were ever rejected tends to support this view. The proportion of

Boys in school infirmary with nurse, 1903.

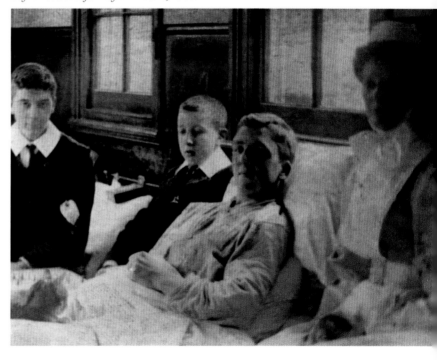

Clockwise from top: *Masters, 1897; Football team, 1890; Monitors, 1887; Masters, 1897.*

FROM LEFT: *Good Conduct certificates, 1888 and 1907; Prize giving programme 1888.*

scholars steadily increased, reaching a pre-war peak in 1912, when LCC scholars formed more than 38 per cent of the total of 562 boys. The downside was that the LCC paid a fee for these scholars which, the inspectors pointed out in 1910, was below the cost of the education given by the school. On top of this, the school also completely exempted from fees 40 boys selected from the parishes of Westminster and Chelsea.

As in many grammar schools, few boys either stayed for long at Emanuel or went on to higher education before the First World War. Of the 100 leavers in 1909–10, three-quarters left Emanuel between the ages of 12 and 17. The first reference to an Oxford scholarship comes in 1894 but the boy in question, L R M Strachan, had moved from Emanuel to Merchant Taylors'. It was not an unusual practice at the time for some parents to use one secondary school as a preparatory school for another they regarded as more appropriate. The first Oxbridge scholarship to a boy who completed his education at Emanuel was awarded in 1908, when R Lumb received the closed Dacre scholarship to Keble College, Oxford. The next did not follow until 1917 when G A Lydward

Front cover of the first school magazine, 1892, renamed The Portcullis, *in 1893.*

Magazine cover, 1910.

gained a choral scholarship to St John's, Cambridge. While only a handful of boys stayed until they were 18, several of them followed distinguished careers, such as A S Ferguson, who became professor of moral philosophy at Durham. More typical was the stream of boys in the 1890s who left to take up clerkships in commerce and the civil service. The inspectors noted in 1910 that most boys found their way into 'offices and various business firms'. This did an injustice to the range of careers taken up by Old Emanuels, as former pupils were known. In 1904, for instance, Old Emanuels were found as surveyors, bank clerks, chemists, dentists and doctors, at home and overseas. The first Old Emanuel Association, formed in 1892, proved short lived but was revived in 1904.

It did not help that Towsey, the first Headmaster, genial, passionate and impulsive, was not a good judge of character and made a number of poor staff appointments. The governors felt that Towsey, who was absent through ill-health, should consider his position. But before he could resign the strain of running the school had proved too much for Towsey. Plagued by financial worries as well as staffing problems, he was dead within two weeks of the governors' meeting.

His successor was the Reverend Arthur Chilton, a 33-year-old Oxford classicist, curate of Holy Trinity in Upper Chelsea. He was a kindly, scholarly man, interested in music. Unlike his predecessor, who once wielded the cane with such vigour that he wore himself out, Chilton rarely used corporal punishment. But the governors had chosen as Headmaster another young man prone to ill-health. One governor, Carey Foster, Principal of University College, London, referring to Chilton's approach as Head, described his 'aspiration for educational peace and quietness and his deprecation of revolution'. He became

Reverend Arthur Chilton, Headmaster 1894–1905.

increasingly distant from the boys even though he professed a great interest in their welfare. Respected by his staff, he perhaps lacked the strength and the urgency to make the improvements the school needed after such a rocky start. He did superintend the construction of the new laboratories in 1898, funded by the Technical Education Board (TEB), which had responsibility for education in London until the LCC assumed its powers in 1904.

Chilton was also handicapped, like Towsey, by a shortage of money. He wanted to pay better salaries to his staff, not only because they had been poorly paid for years, but also because he needed to attract better-quality teachers if there was to be any marked improvement in

Arthur Chilton with pupils and his son, 1897.

ABOVE: *Reverend Harold Buchanan Ryley, Headmaster 1905–13 with choir, and* (BELOW) *with prefects.* BOTTOM: *A chemistry laboratory, 1898.*

examination results. But it was only at the very end of his headship, as the school started receiving grants from the Board of Education and the LCC, that the governors felt able to relax their grip on the purse strings and approve a new scheme of staff allowances. The school became so reliant on LCC funding that in 1908 it was reckoned that without it Emanuel would have been in deficit. The flow of income from the state made it possible to improve teaching conditions for the first time in years. The new classrooms and other work spaces provided during that year were long overdue and certainly met an urgent need.

Chilton departed in the summer of 1905 to become Headmaster of the City of London School. The vacancy at Emanuel attracted wide interest and the shortlist included candidates from University College School, Highgate, Westminster, Tonbridge and Rossall. But there was only one man with previous experience as a Head. Harold Buchanan Ryley was another young man, aged 36, another Oxford classicist and another clergyman. Widowed with two sons, he had taught in the US and since 1901 had been Headmaster of Sir Roger Manwood's Grammar School, Sandwich, in charge of 320 boys. He won the post by eleven votes to six from the other

outstanding candidate, the senior science master from Westminster.

Ryley was a much more vigorous Head than either Towsey or Chilton. He was warm and inspiring but also impulsive and volatile, qualities which led him into repeated conflict with the governors. A man of immense energy, he set himself such ambitious aims that, without any secretarial support, he often suffered from nervous exhaustion brought on by overwork. A man of vision, he had little patience for details, which proved to be a terminal weakness. High-minded and idealistic, he declared at prize giving in 1909 that his ambition was 'to make Emanuel one of the greatest of London schools, not only by organizing the scheme of instruction with the aid of increased classroom accommodation and apparatus, but by the development of that spirit of sacrificing self for the good of the whole, which is the characteristic of Public School life'. Two years later he expounded that

the old name of school, domus, our home, our house, expressed what should be our ideal today, whether we belonged to the greater public schools or to one of the other secondary schools of the country. School was a place in which boys learnt to live a corporate life … in an organism to which each boy owed duties and service … It should even hold up a high ideal of manly living and of unselfish devotion to the Commonwealth, and its members should know that the highest thing they can say is that they have done their duty to England.

This was all in tune with the times, the heyday of Empire, the Edwardian interlude between victory achieved in the South African War and the carnage yet to be experienced in the First World War. Ryley was expressing what the guest of honour that year, Baden-Powell, the founder of the Scouts and probably the most famous man in the country, stated in rather simpler

terms: 'A boy had to learn such things as honour, honesty and self-reliance, and not drift into being a sneak, but stand true and upright. Boys had to learn to be gentlemen, and a gentleman was not judged by the money in his pocket, but by his conduct. They should be chivalrous and help others along. This had to be done by oneself.' (This did not cut much ice with the school's debating society which resolved a little later that 'the Boy Scout movement does not justify its existence'.)

The inspectors, visiting the school just months after Ryley took over, applauded his aims. They concluded their report by stating that

the school at present is in a transition stage. The Headmaster has been so recently appointed that as yet he has not been able to overcome the difficulties that undoubtedly exist. The prevalent inertia and want of tone can only be removed by firmness, by increased definiteness of aim among the staff,

and by a systematized and thorough attempt to interest and stimulate the boys ... The intellectual and moral standard both need raising.

This was clearly apparent to Ryley who spent time assessing the teaching in the school during early 1906. He set about shaking up the staff, raising expectations and improving standards. New and better-qualified masters, such as Charles Hills in 1908, with his first-class Oxford degree, produced a steady improvement in examination results from 1909 onwards. With an eye to stimulating academic achievement while ensuring that the education of the majority of the boys was not neglected, he also divided the school into classical and modern sides, later adding a Technical (Commercial and Manual) form. Weekly journals were introduced to record homework and class marks. Most of the library stock was renewed in 1906 and a new library built to house it in 1907. The

Emanuel School, 1902.

school magazine, referring to popular boys' authors of the day, had earlier observed that '60 per cent of Guy Boothby and 30 per cent of Henty are not right proportions for any Library'. The Junior School was reborn in 1910 with a single class of 30 boys aged between six and 11 under one mistress. When the inspectors came back in 1910, they praised the progress made by Ryley in academic work and concluded that 'much good work is being accomplished in all departments of the school, and throughout there is a considerable amount of varied activity, which reflects considerable credit upon the Headmaster and the staff. There is, indeed, every indication that the school promises to become a very important day school'.

The way in which boys were encouraged to make their views known through the magazine was symptomatic of the vigour and vibrancy which Ryley brought to

Geography room, 1907.

Emanuel. There had been extra-curricular activities before he was appointed but they were never extensive and occurred in a haphazard way. Towsey had introduced evening 'entertainments' for the boarders and encouraged cycling and photography. For many years the school choir enjoyed an annual outing, initially to Crystal Palace and then almost invariably to Box Hill. Chilton added lantern lectures and concerts but it was not until Ryley's arrival that activities flourished. Societies were more abundant, there were more visits, usually for boys interested in engineering to places such as Nine Elms Locomotive Depot or the Woolwich Arsenal, and drama was produced for the first time. Music expanded under Hedley 'Bandy' Evans, who had joined the staff in 1888 and served as music master until 1933. The main event was an annual concert, performed by a choir and orchestra made up of staff, past

The new library, 1907.

CLOCKWISE FROM TOP LEFT: *Football team, 1906; Pupil, 1907; Emanuel School RFC, 1908–9.*

and present pupils and friends, usually in the Town Hall. A favourite work, regularly performed, almost too often, was Stanford's *Songs of the Fleet*. In 1906 there was even a film show, although this was severely criticized by the boys because the films were blurred to the point of invisibility. In 1913 the first Hobbies Exhibition was held, with displays of woodwork, model engines, photography, art, picture postcards and cigarette cards, pets and natural history collections.

Ryley had a similar influence on games. At first games concentrated on football and cricket, with organized matches starting in 1887. Although the first rugby house matches were played in the following year, the game was played only spasmodically at the school for the next 20 years. Sporting life revolved around the boarders and matches often involved mixed sides of staff and boys. In the school grounds Gag's Corner, for instance, gained its name from a tremendous six hit by G A Garrington, who joined the staff in 1897 and later became second master. There was also an annual sports day and a fives club was formed in 1896, although it tended to wax and wane over the years. But the day boys, excluded from school competitions, had become too used to joining outside clubs. This all changed under Ryley. The first stimulus to school sport was his creation of a body of form representatives to consider sporting matters. It was this body which was persuaded in 1906 by W W 'Hooky' Parkinson, who joined the staff in 1901, to adopt rugby as a school sport, a decision ratified by the entire school. The first

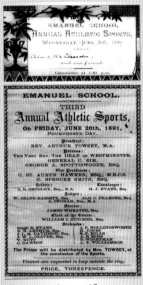

TOP: *Sporting certificate.*
ABOVE: *Sports day programme.*

inter-school match was against the City of London School which Emanuel won 13–0. Rugby was played in the Michaelmas term and soccer in Lent. A report on the early fortunes of the school rugby teams in 1906 noted that the lack of success achieved by the second and third XVs was largely because their numbers on match days were weakened by the absence of those held in detention. The school's first-ever first XV included George Hirst, who later played for Wales. The range of physical activities increased, covering drill, gymnastics, shooting, cricket, rugby, football, boxing, fencing, running, cycling, water polo and swimming (another improvement was heating the swimming bath from 1907 onwards), so that, declared *The Portcullis*, 'we ought to hear no more of Emanuel boys playing for outside clubs'. (*The Portcullis* is the school magazine, dating back to 1893.) The school timetable was altered to make time for games, the Magdalen ground was hired to provide extra cricket pitches 'with real grass on them' and the gym was renovated to allow the introduction of a systematic course of Physical Education. In 1912 school matches in swimming and cross-country were held for the first

ABOVE: *Pupils by the school gate.* BELOW: *House mistress with junior house boys, 1909.*

Cricket, 1908. (S G Parkes, the recipient of the swimming certificate below, is in the centre of the photograph.)

time. Most importantly, perhaps, was the founding of the rowing club in 1913, when a Russian pupil, Treshatny, and his friends took a four onto the river at Putney. The first match was rowed against Kingston Grammar School over the Borough Regatta course on 16 July 1914 – Emanuel won.

Another fillip given to games by Ryley, which also had an impact throughout the school, was the formation of houses. The suggestion had actually come from the school inspectors in 1906, as a way of bringing boarders and day boys closer together and encouraging a greater interest by the latter in school games. So the school magazine noted that

Swimming certificate awarded to S G Parkes in his final year at Emanuel, 1910.

summer that 'the dormitory competition has been changed to a house competition. Instead of having a representative day-boy team to play among the dormitories, the whole school had been divided into houses'. Five were formed – Marlborough, Wellington, Lyons, Clyde and Howe. They took their names from those of the military heroes first painted on the doors of the original dormitories when the buildings had been used as an orphanage. House spirit extended to other activities, with inter-house concerts and house teas, but it would be true to say that sport, with the corps, dominated house life. In 1908

Howe became the first house to have only day boys while Drake was added in 1910 and Rodney and Nelson were formed as junior houses in 1911. At the same time the dormitory monitors, whose privileges included bacon or sausage at breakfast and leave from the grounds on half-days, were replaced by prefects, with powers of

TOP: *Marlborough House first XI, 1907. Marlborough was one of the first houses introduced by Ryley – sporting rivalry between houses was intense from the very start.*
MIDDLE: *A selection of sporting trophies dating from 1906.* LEFT: *House rugby shield, initially competed for as the dormitory shield in 1888.*

punishment, initially restricted to setting impositions for minor offences. Corporal punishment was restricted to the Headmaster until the end of 1914 when Ryley's successor, Shirley Goodwin, authorized its use by assistant masters.

The cadet corps was introduced in the same year as houses made their first appearance, although there had been military drill at the school since it had opened. A rifle range was completed in 1904 and the school's rifle club became affiliated to the National Rifle Association in 1905. The corps began as Z Company, the Queen's Westminster Volunteers, with 82 members, but became part of the Officers' Training Corps (OTC) in 1909. Gilbert Burnett, who had joined the staff in 1905, took charge. He was given the rank of captain in 1914 and retired from command as a major in 1927. By the summer of 1914, the Emanuel OTC had 195 members plus another 80 in a subsidiary company, accounting for almost half the boys in the school.

Undeniably Ryley did much to improve the school. It was unfortunate that he left the school in 1913 for the departure of such a strong leader surely contributed in part to the difficulties the school endured in the decade to come. But in his constant battles with the governors over the boundaries of his authority there could only ever be one winner and when another such crisis arose in 1913 the governors had had enough. Ryley was asked to resign. His departure was much lamented by those outside the board of governors. In charting his achievements, the growth in numbers, recognition by the Board of Education, the house system and the prefects, the OTC, school societies and expansion in sporting opportunities, the school magazine concluded that 'there is a chance for every boy to follow his particular bent and in no other school is so much done for the average boy'.

Shirley Goodwin was appointed from a shortlist of seven, whittled down from 140 applications, in October 1913. He was young, aged only 33, and married without children. Another classicist, educated at University College School and Balliol College, Oxford, he was the first non-clergyman to hold the Headship and the first not to act as chaplain, although he was personally devout. At the time of his appointment he was Headmaster of Glasgow High School with 866 pupils. But it seems

Emanuel joined the Officer Training Corps (OTC) in 1909. The OTC was a major feature of school life, remembered by generations of OEs.

Classroom scene, 1912.

Shirley Goodwin, Headmaster 1914–27, with Betty, his beloved Scottie dog.

strange that the governors, after their experience with Towsey, Chilton and Ryley, should give the post to another man who suffered from ill-health. His Oxford degree was an aegrotat degree, awarded to a student absent through ill-health from examinations.

At first Goodwin seemed intent on making his mark on the school. In June 1914 he told the governors that he proposed dividing the school into Junior (7–10), Middle (10–13) and Senior (13–18) Schools. The Senior School in turn would be divided into several sides – Classical, Modern, Army, Scientific and Colonial or Manual. With the first two aimed at boys with university ambitions as well as those intending to pursue commerce or the professions, he described the last as 'for adaptable boys of that stamp'. He intended to raise the standard of the entrance exam and institute tests for boys passing from one part of the school to the next, using his discretion to exclude those he deemed unsuitable at each stage. Games and drill would become compulsory.

But his plans were swept aside by the First World War. As with many other similar schools, the school magazine was filled with letters written at the front by former pupils. One, who had been a house captain and prefect, urged every boy to join the OTC for his belief was that they would all be needed since 'the war will last years'. Old Emanuels were decorated, the first award being the Military Cross to Lieutenant Leslie Clinton. And then the list of the dead and wounded began to appear, growing longer and longer. Among the first to fall from Emanuel were A A Hunt, a sergeant with the Canadian Expeditionary Force, W T Damen of the 23rd Battalion, London Regiment, H E Woodward of the Artists' Rifles, and a young man named Poole, serving on board HMS *Cressy*. In a way the censors in a later world war would never permit, men wrote of their yearning for promised leave as a respite from the trenches, others described the terrifying nature of modern trench warfare and the horror of going over the top. In 1916, when the deaths of the two brothers, Ronald and Cecil Grundy, sons of a future Headmaster were recorded, G E Hopwood wrote that 'it is difficult, very difficult at times, to believe that this futile, squabbling life of ours is part of a great destiny, that an Infinite Wisdom watches compassionately over us at all'.

William Frank Godfrey, 1896–1916, was one of at least 170 OEs to lose his life in the First World War. He died at the Battle of the Somme, along with eight other OEs.

Stanley A George Harvey, 1893–1918, affectionately known as SAG to his friends, was a true Emanuel character. He wrote hundreds of letters to the school during the war. They were published in the 'From the Trenches' pages of The Portcullis magazine. Sadly, he was killed towards the end of the war.

Edmund Fisher was killed in 1916 only two terms after leaving school. He was, remembered his school friend A E Titley, 'the hero of that epoch ... a giant of six foot three, who captained an unbeaten rugby team, made several athletics records and was a senior prefect'. Joseph Deeks was one of the boys present at the announcement of Fisher's death: 'we felt the tragedy of war every week, for at daily service in the school chapel, we heard of the death of some Emanuelite serving in the front line'. The first XV of 1912–13 was shattered by the war, with eight dead, one missing and three wounded. In 1917 the school's former Head, H B Ryley, lost both his sons, one a former school captain of Emanuel, and then, accepted for the services himself, lost his own life in Palestine. By the end of the war Emanuel, based on the available figures, had lost a higher proportion of former pupils on active service than any other school. The authors of a previous history of the school calculated that 139 of the 815 Old Emanuels who served with the forces never returned home.

At Emanuel concerts were cancelled, visits curtailed, matches called off and fives abandoned (fives balls became unobtainable when the makers produced munitions instead). The Head assumed command of the OTC which had risen to 310 strong by the end of 1914. For a week the War Office

FROM LEFT: *Commissioned officers, First World War; First World War Memorial in the chapel; Two OTC cadets in front of the memorial.*

*Two sides of a postcard. On one side is the Emanuel School first XV of 1912–13, and on the other side is
the fate that befell them in the war. Sixth from the right on the back row is H B Ryley, the school captain in 1914 and the youngest son
of the Headmaster, H Buchanan Ryley. Ryley lost both his sons in the trenches and was killed himself in Palestine in 1917. Out of the team, eight were
killed, three were wounded and one is marked as missing in action. Second from right on the front row is Leslie Stuart Clinton, the first OE to be awarded
the Military Cross. The senior school house rugby competition was named after him and pupils today still contest the Clinton Cup.*

authorized the OTC to keep watch over railway lines in case of saboteurs but this came to an end because the boys could not be issued with live ammunition. The Sergeant-Instructor, Meacher, left to rejoin his old regiment in 1916 and later died on active service. At the request of the Woolwich Arsenal, the school itself set up a small munitions workshop, operated by boys during the day and by Old Emanuels at night. Munitions production even claimed the school boathouse and it took some time for the rowing club to find an alternative base in Hammersmith. Wheat to make bread was grown on the school fields, followed later by turnips, carrots, cabbages, sprouts and broccoli. Boys were sent on harvest camps up to Hexham in Northumberland. Speech

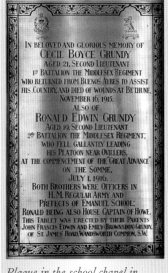

Plaque in the school chapel in memory of the Grundy brothers.

Day continued, with guests later in the war attending undeterred by fear of the Zeppelins which had taken to raiding London, although plain certificates took the place of bound books for prizes. The War Office briefly considered commandeering the school as a convalescent hospital in 1916. Teaching suffered because staff were called up and rarely replaced while the buildings suffered since repairs and maintenance became all but impossible through the shortage of men and materials. All this disturbed school life, creating during Christmas Term 1917 what was described in the school magazine as 'an indescribable current of unrest'.

1919–1939
A New Broom

The war sapped Goodwin's energy and accelerated his decline in health. Saddened by the deaths of so many he had known, overwhelmed by the effort of keeping the school going almost on his own, depressed by the dilapidated condition of the school buildings, he was never the same man. The consequences were clear from the school inspection which took place in 1920. This highlighted the poor state of the buildings, the way too many pupils had been admitted too rapidly in an effort to sustain the school's cash flow, the resulting discontent among staff and the burden upon the Head, and the distance of the governors from the school. The inspectors could only conclude that 'at the present time Emanuel was not a good school'. Initial attempts to resolve these problems met with little success. An ambitious reconstruction scheme submitted to the LCC for grant aid fell on deaf ears. Minor improvements were made but clearly more was needed. Even in 1929, when Charles Hill joined the staff, he found that rats would pop up through the gaps in the floorboards in the dining hall, foraging for scraps, the OTC sergeant-major taking pot-shots at them with a .22 rifle. The head no longer had the energy to raise academic expectations and his health continued to deteriorate.

Staff and senior boys on Flannels Day, 1922. Shirley Goodwin is wearing a striped blazer.

CLOCKWISE FROM ABOVE: *The school song,* Pour Bien Desirer, *was first published in 1916; Shirley Goodwin with prefects, 1919. W Stafford Hipkins, sitting on left, and J B C Grundy, on the ground, both returned to the school after university. Grundy became Headmaster in 1953 and when he left, Hipkins, who had served for many years as second master, became acting Headmaster; Miss Wagstaff with Form 2. She was one of the first female teachers to have her own year group, 1918.*

Numbers began to fall. Financial problems became more acute. Although the LCC had been persuaded by 1925 to renew its funding, taking over the staff salaries bill, the governors were faced in 1926 with the decision of the Board of Education to withdraw its grant. This left the school hoping that the gap would be covered by extra funding from the LCC. An unforeseen consequence of total reliance for grant aid on the LCC was the question mark it would place over the status of the school some years hence. But there were some bright spots. Goodwin formed the Dacre Society as an umbrella organization for several activities, such as philately, numismatics, engineering and natural history, followed in 1923 by the junior version, the Sackville Club. Both of them ebbed and flowed according to schoolboy fashion, the Dacre Society becoming the Dacre Club in the late 1920s as a discussion group for the upper school before being

revived under its original name in the mid-1930s. Rowing enjoyed a purple patch. The first IV reached the final of the Public Schools Challenge Cup at the Marlow Regatta in 1921 and 1922, the first school eight was raised in 1922 and by the mid-1920s was racing against – and often beating – students from UCL, Imperial College and the LSE, as well as pacing one of the Varsity crews every year. There were a handful of Oxbridge scholarships, notably the senior scholarship to Trinity College, Cambridge, won by Owen Saunders, later vice-chancellor of the University of London, in 1924.

In the same year the Old Emanuel Association (OEA) and the Old Emanuel Rugby Football Club, encouraged by Goodwin, discussed the acquisition of additional playing fields. These would provide headquarters for the rugby club, facilities for other Old Emanuel sporting activities and more space for the school. The OEA secretary, F H White, came across Blagdons Farm, near Raynes Park, in June 1924, a large house with an orchard and 14 acres of meadowland in a state of some neglect. More than 300 Old Emanuels covenanted funds and in July 1925 the governing body acquired the property for £4,340 (around £175,000 today). The land was littered with tree stumps and concrete foundations, and a deep tree-lined ditch ran parallel with the Beverley Brook across the field. The arterial road now forming one boundary had not been constructed. The putative changing rooms were dilapidated stables with other decaying buildings on the site of what became the car park. A tangle of grass in summer, it was a swamp in winter. A groundsman was appointed, the house renovated, the stables converted into changing rooms, and large water tanks for a water supply and baths, showers and hot water installed. The ground was cleared and in October 1925 the junior teams of the Old Emanuel RFC were playing on two rough and ready pitches. A fund was opened to raise money to improve the ground, with Old Emanuels forming labour squads each weekend. The Old Emanuel Cricket and Tennis Clubs were formed in summer 1926 although there was no

Cyril Broom, Headmaster 1927–53. Second master, George Wyatt, became acting Head in 1927 after the sudden death of Shirley Goodwin.

suitable square and the grass courts were patchy and uneven. After initial clearance work done by the OEA, contractors levelled and drained the ground, the cost being met equally by the OEA and the governing body. The ditch was also filled in. Three pitches were marked out and over the winter of 1926–7 a cricket square was laid. En-tout-cas constructed a hard tennis court in the spring of 1927 and a new water supply was laid on. The rugby club also paid for the cost of installing electricity in the house, something the school still lacked.

The first cricket match played on the new square at Blagdons occurred in May 1927. In the following month Goodwin died at school. He was only 47. The second master, George Wyatt, led the school from the end of the summer term in 1927 until the arrival of Goodwin's successor in the summer term of the following year. In October 1927 the governors appointed Cyril Broom as Headmaster. Like Goodwin and Ryley, Broom was already a Headmaster. Coming to Emanuel, he obviously liked a challenge. He had been Headmaster of Colfe's Grammar School, another ancient London educational foundation, since 1924. The governors must have been impressed with his achievements at Colfe's. He had

BELOW LEFT: *OE sports team at Blagdons.* RIGHT: *School play,* The Captives, *1922.*

brought fresh ideas in organization and management. He had developed a large and diverse sixth form, generating more entrants for the Higher School Certificate and more university scholarships. He had expanded the school's social activities, through lectures, concerts, plays and excursions. He had been eager to see the boys had as much sporting choice as possible, so against his better instincts he retained soccer while introducing rugby. He was keen on the development of good manners, politeness and courtesy, smartness of appearance and what Colfe's historian described as 'a uniformity of school dress'. He had worked closely with the Old Boys and with parents, introducing parents' evenings. As numbers rose, he had taken the lead in planning new buildings. Above all he believed, the school history recorded, 'in the school as a corporate family, with interests beyond those in ordinary school hours'.

There were no quick fixes in turning around Emanuel but Broom knew there were things he could do straightaway to create a better impression. A long list of small but effective reforms took place during his first couple of years. He modernized the curriculum, adding Spanish, economics, more German and geography. He gave every boy the chance to play sport at least once a week and persuaded the governors to fund rugby and cricket properly rather than relying on masters to spend

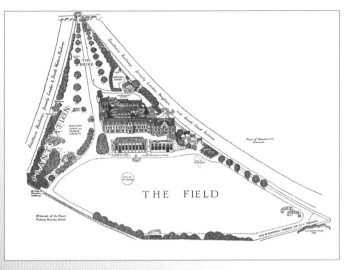

THE FIELD

THIS AND FACING PAGE: *Past and present members of Emanuel took part in 'Beating the Bounds' on Flannels Day. The ceremony was steeped in tradition and much fun was had as the procession moved around the school's boundary visiting landmarks such as the Tall Man, the site of the Mound, Gag's Corner and the pigsty (see map). The proceedings were led by the Public Orator (in this instance an OE, C W Giles) wearing a false beard and academic costume. In front of him dressed in white sheets and clutching symbols of their position are the Ushers of the Rugger Pill, Cricket Bat, Tennis Racquet, Hockey Stick, Golf Club, Detention Book and Cane.*

The Public Orator: 'You see before you the Gates of Emanuel School… How often have you run the length of this Drive, only to be in time to sign the Late Book! How often have you, as boarders, climbed that wall, to pay surreptitious visits to the Tuck Shops on Battersea Rise! Friends, this spot is hallowed for you and for me by many joyous memories …I declare you to be the gates of Emanuel School. May you stand for ever!
Yonder wall conceals from our view an iron track which I declare to be the London, Brighton and South Coast railway. Yonder fence reveals the London and South Western Railway … I declare wall and fence to be boundaries of our drive and let none venture over them … but may your trains be fitted with silencers, and your tracks be made of rubber, that our peace may be less disturbed.'

By a 'keep off the grass' sign:
'And let no one tear out or wrench off this elegantly worded notice, as was done in aforetime by evil minded boys …'

By the site of the old infirmary:
'O the fights that have taken place in yonder corner, where your walls formed a hidden and convenient arena! O how many boys have lain doggo in your shadow, when they should have been on the Corps Parade! My friends, weep upon that patch of earth, and perchance the grass may grow greener for your weeping.
But as for me, my task is done. Whip me that boy that he may remember these things … the bounds of this School have been well and truly beaten, as this unfortunate youth shall witness as long as he shall live.'

Of course, the boy in this case was only ceremonially whipped and the whole ceremony was tongue-in-cheek.

Emanuel School, painted before the steeple on the tower was taken down in 1931.

their own money. He introduced with great success receptions for parents and insisted they should agree that their sons should stay at Emanuel for a minimum of four years. He revived extra-curricular activities, arranging lectures and recitals, encouraging the formation of new societies, such as the League of Nations Union, the Natural History Society, the Christian Union, the Carey-Foster Society for furthering the knowledge of science and the Dorset Society as a literary and debating society for fifth formers. He and his wife took 21 boys on the school's first overseas visit, to a Spanish camp at Vigo during the summer of 1928. A little later, in 1931, he introduced a standard uniform, unimpressed with the vague regulations that produced 'a great and undesirable variety of colour and quality in clothing'. He got together a committee of prefects and staff which recommended a uniform of either a black jacket and vest with dark-striped trousers or grey flannel suit with a dark blue overcoat or mackintosh. Improvements in academic performance, staff and buildings were his long-term goals. Although the pass rate for the School Certificate in

1929 was 78 per cent, this was the success rate for those boys entered for the exam, not for all boys who were eligible. Only four obtained the Higher Certificate. Too many boys – about half – were still leaving without achieving the School Certificate. Firstly Broom set out to reform the admissions procedure. He appears to have encountered resistance from the governors but another critical report from the inspectors in 1929 gave him the evidence to convince them that higher admission and promotion standards should be introduced. He had already insisted that LCC scholars would be accepted only after re-examination by the school.

Secondly, he began to rejuvenate the staff. Again he had the inspectors on his side. They applauded his appointments of younger staff who became mainly responsible for the best teaching in the school. Wherever possible, Broom sought to appoint men with first-class or upper-second-class degrees, preferably Oxbridge scholarship holders. He did not hesitate to recruit externally for senior appointments, such as G B H Jones as senior history master and F H Dowler as sixth form classical master in 1930. Others included men like Charles Hill, who became a stalwart of the school until his retirement in 1964. He was not only a respected teacher, developing the advanced sixth form course in geography. He was also housemaster of Marlborough for

BELOW: *Aerial view of Emanuel School from the 1930s and* (MAIN PICTURE) *2005.*

over 30 years and took a leading role in a wide range of school activities, from the OTC and shooting to drama, rowing, fives and overseas trips. The inspectors did single out existing members of staff for praise. They pinpointed the senior English staff, W Stafford 'Hippy' Hipkins, the head of department, and his partner, Harry 'Dolly' Mearns. Hipkins had been at Emanuel as a boy, joined the staff in 1921, gained his degree part-time in 1923 and was senior English master from 1926 until 1947, retiring in 1964. He was such a loyal servant of the school he was said to have been conceived in the grounds. A real gentleman, softly spoken, impeccably courteous, he was an ideal secretary of the common room, which, recorded the school magazine, was 'a post requiring no small tact when the staff were divided into two, known as the Lords and the Commons'. The phrase neatly described the division of the common room between those staff who worked but had no need to and those who worked because they had to. Mearns was a complete contrast, sharp-tongued and outspoken, a man who did not suffer fools gladly yet was often helpful and kindly. On the staff from 1920 until 1967, he was particularly involved with drama and music. He was a scholarly musician whose collection of early Mozart editions he bequeathed to the British Museum. Hedley Evans, the music master and probably the oldest member of staff, who would retire after 45 years in 1933, was also singled out for his fresh and enthusiastic approach and his receptiveness to change.

But there were still too many weak spots on the staff; too much teaching was leisurely and the general standard of work was not very good. As a result, the governors decided to enforce the retirement of four staff and asked the Headmaster to make recommendations in future for the retirement of any staff over 60. Broom was unhesitating throughout the 1930s in removing under-performing staff wherever possible and replacing them with a string of men who made their mark on the school. They included C J 'Bill' Hyde, who came to teach Latin and Greek in 1931, became a housemaster, games master and secretary

MAIN PICTURE: *Scene from* The Mikado, *1937. The producer, Harry Mearns, taught at Emanuel for 47 years.* FROM LEFT: The Mikado, *1937; two scenes from* The Rivals, *1925;* Cox and Box, *1935;* HMS Pinafore, *1936; a selection of programmes.*

of the common room, a humane, tolerant and civilized man. W Claude 'Taffy' Neath arrived early in 1936 to join Hyde in teaching classics. He also taught French, coached rugby and cricket, became games master, went on to serve with distinction in the Second World War and later chaired the common room. In 1930 the governors had agreed that modern studies, with an emphasis on modern languages, instead of classics, should be the focus of the school. Owen Ginn, known as Boozey Ginn, taught French innovatively by the direct method, expecting only French to be spoken in the classroom. Emanuel gained a national reputation for the quality of its French teaching through its great success in the *Grand Concours* of the *Société Nationale des Professeurs de Français en Angleterre*, being the top school in the country in 1937 and 1938. Another innovation in languages also came in 1937, when Emanuel was one of the first London schools to teach Russian in the sixth form, under Mr Loewenson. Also in 1937 Aeron Rogers, another Welshman, joined the school to teach mathematics. Rogers was an outstanding mathematician, with first-class degrees from the University of Wales and from Balliol College, Oxford. Hard-working, committed, resolute, he revitalized an ailing department before the war and established its high reputation after the war with a string of scholarship successes. Hugely respected, commanding silence simply by appearing or with a twitch of his immense bushy eyebrows, he had the gift of drawing out the academic potential of his pupils, whom he divided in class between the Scholars and the Gentlemen. Many former pupils would testify to his life-changing influence.

Many of these newcomers were impressed with the man who appointed him. According to Neath, Broom was a man with 'a razor-sharp mind', a fondness for alliteration (such as his reference to 'Tooting toughs') and a knowledge of every boy in the school. Broom obviously impressed his peers as well for he was elected to the Headmasters' Conference in 1933. Through keeping the best of the old

The Needham Trophies for house athletics.

while recruiting new talent, he steadily raised the school's academic results. In 1935 more than half of all those leaving at 16, not just those entered for the examinations, passed their School Certificate. This may not sound impressive but ten years earlier the pass rate among all leavers was just 15 per cent. Broom encouraged boys in an age before university grants or loans to consider higher education by urging the governors to establish more leaving exhibitions in the belief that 'no greater asset towards the object of gaining recognition as a Public School can be obtained than an adequate supply of Leaving Exhibitions'. He also believed strongly that as soon as a boy stepped through the school gates and began the long walk down the drive, he became the complete responsibility of the school. When one parent withdrew his son from the school in 1931 in protest at the school's system of discipline, Broom was unperturbed, stating that 'the boy cannot profit by the intellectual education if the development of his character is to be retarded by parental interference'.

But Broom was far from hostile to parents. They were more often seen around the school than they had ever been in the past. From the success of the parents' receptions came, at his suggestion, the formation of the Parents' Association in July 1933, which held meetings on a variety of topics, such as physical education, health and careers. Health was still a matter of great concern to parents. Before the introduction of antibiotics, death still crept up unawares on the young and the school magazine recorded several instances of sudden deaths from pneumonia, tuberculosis and meningitis, while outbreaks of measles and scarlet fever were not uncommon.

As a result of Broom's reforms, numbers began to rise and boys joining Emanuel during the 1930s were there on merit, not because the school was desperate to take them. They were also there because their parents could overlook the poor physical condition of the school and see a more vibrant institution, with a talented and committed staff, under the leadership of

Harvest Festival in the chapel.

a strong Headmaster, whose results were steadily improving. In 1934, for instance, 149 candidates from 39 schools applied for the 11 special free places available at the school in open competition for boys from Battersea and Wandsworth. In February 1939 the school roll stood at 578, with 214 LCC scholars, 63 Special Foundation Scholars and 22 Foundation Scholars. Fee payers accounted for less than half the school. Emanuel really was carrying out Lady Dacre's wishes to educate poor children.

The vibrancy of Emanuel was seen in the ever-expanding provision of sporting opportunities and other school activities, in which new members of staff played a key role. From the late 1920s until the late 1930s, groups of boys variously accompanied Mr Hill to the Lake District, Wales and the Austrian Tyrol, Mr Bond to Germany, Mr Hughes and Mr Camfield on cruises around the Baltic, and Messrs Ginn, Mearns and Camfield to Paris. Just before the outbreak of war, there were also two exchange visits with a German school, the

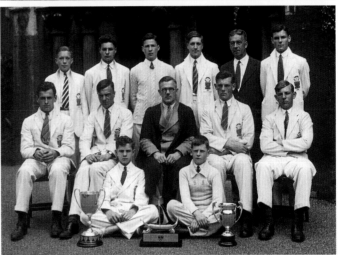

MAIN PICTURE: *The school's rowing tank, officially opened by Steve Fairbarn in 1929.* TOP: *Alpha Fours winning crew, 1937.* ABOVE: *Emanuel School boats club had an excellent season in 1935. Shown here with the Headmaster, Cyril Broom, seated and their coach, James Worth, standing.*

Realgymnasium in Bremen. Claude Neath helped to raise the standard of rugby. He remembered that before the war the school pack was huge, full of young men over six feet in height and 13 stones in weight, who then rowed during the summer with the school four. In 1933 the school had at last won the Public School Fours, held at the Reading Regatta, under their coach, James Worth. Emanuel repeated the feat in 1935, also winning the fours at Twickenham Regatta. By then, the school had moved from Auriol boathouse at Hammersmith to train on the river at Barnes where the facilities were much better. The school was racing mainly in clinker fours or tub fours, lacking a decent eight until a new one arrived in 1938, by which time Mr Lee was in charge of coaching. Under

The Ashburton shooting team with Captain Hill, 1935.

Harry Mearns, school drama productions expanded in scope, ranging from Shakespeare through Molière and Sheridan to Wilde and Shaw. Musical performance, however, was something of a weak spot after the departure of Hedley Evans. Musical productions still

relied on staff and former pupils although the school was becoming more ambitious by the end of the decade, moving away from the works of minor 19th-century English composers and at last tackling great pieces of music such as Haydn's *Creation*. Goodwin's Dacre Society had become the Dacre Club before Broom arrived but enjoyed the mixed fortunes of many school societies and was revived again in 1935.

Where Broom had less success was in his plans for reconstructing the school. In 1929, when the inspectors came to call, the school was full of small rooms, with an inadequate hall, poorly lit corridors, dark and unheated cloakrooms, peeling plaster, rising floors, falling ceilings, and a dingy chapel with a derelict organ. In May 1930 the UWF Clerk wrote to the LCC, pointing out the deficiencies of the buildings, listing a new hall, new gym and electrification as minimum requirements, and noting that further urgent internal repairs and refurbishment were required. This list, estimated in total to cost £20,000 (some £900,000 today), was a far cry from the ambitious £70,000 programme advocated by Goodwin. But these

Emanuel boys at Kingsdown Camp, Subsidiary Corps, 1935.

OTC 1931 with Stuart Surridge (third from left) and John Galsworthy (fifth from left). Surridge went on to captain the Surrey cricket team and Galsworthy became a respected diplomat.

were different times from the immediate post-war years and education had been and would again be subject to cutbacks in government spending in light of the economic crises which bedevilled the British economy. The governors obviously thought the LCC would be more amenable to their current plans. At the end of 1930 one governor wondered whether the buildings were worth all the trouble and suggested relocating the school but this idea had been discounted by the following summer. Nothing happened – except the removal of the unsafe spire from the central tower in 1931. But three years later Broom and his architect, G F Turner, submitted a five-year building plan, concentrated heavily on repairing, refurbishing and modernizing the existing buildings, combined with a new hall, new gym, new science labs, new pavilion and boathouse. The chapel was brought back into use and in 1936 the restoration of the organ was celebrated with a recital by George Thalben-Ball. In the next year, eight years after Broom had first made the suggestion and 34 years after the governors had

first considered the idea, electric lighting was installed. The school magazine reported that 'the school at night resembles a peculiarly brilliant constellation'. With a new hall and gym built at the same time, it was a momentous

Practising first aid at Kingsdown.

ABOVE: *In the shadow of impending war: Old Emanuel Association, 29th annual dinner at the Café Royal, London, 1938. Headmaster Cyril Broom (with glasses) is seated in the middle of the rectangular table with Frank Abbott, Chairman of the Governors, on his left.* FACING PAGE: *The new gym and Hampden Hall were opened by Viscount Hampden in 1937. In the same year the school finally entered the modern age by replacing its antiquated gas lighting with electric lighting.*

year for Emanuel. The hall, named the Hampden Hall, and the gym were both opened by Viscount Hampden, a descendant of Lady Dacre, on 4 November 1937.

A year later the optimism for the future of Emanuel exemplified by the opening of the new buildings began to seem premature. The school magazine recorded at Christmas 1938 that 'the first indication of any likelihood of world catastrophe was foreshadowed by a parents' meeting, during which the possibility of evacuation was thoroughly discussed. Events moved so quickly after this that within three days the school was in a position to leave London at short notice'. But beyond rehearsal the crisis subsided and the school resumed normality. Gas masks, kit bags and tinned food all disappeared. It was only a temporary respite. In the late summer of 1939 Emanuel found itself once again at war.

The school was evacuated to Churcher's College in Petersfield, Hampshire at the beginning of the Second World War. This is the Market Square in Petersfield in the 1930s, painted by local artist Flora Twort.

5

1939–1953

From War to Peace

At 11.15am on Friday 1 September, two days before war was declared, a special train left Clapham Junction, carrying 444 boys from Emanuel School into exile. The boys had no idea where they were going until the train stopped at the Hampshire market town of Petersfield. They made their way from the station to the parish church where, under the direction of Aeron Rogers, they were allocated billets. Peter Knottley and his brother, for instance, were sent to stay with the kindly and understanding Mr and Mrs Wickens. Some householders accepted several boys while one woman, having volunteered to take eight small girls, never batted an eyelid when eight burly members of the upper school turned up instead. For many boys, their billets became second homes and their hosts their friends.

The next morning everyone met at Churcher's College which generously hosted Emanuel throughout the war. Books and supplies were brought down in vans from London and school began on 20 September. The train had also brought 50 younger brothers of Emanuel boys who attended local elementary schools. Churcher's, while happy to share its accommodation and playing fields, simply did not have enough space for the whole of Emanuel. Instead, rooms were taken at the Working

the OTC featured in church parades and the Old Emanuels brought down a team to play against local opposition.

The boys quickly settled in but their Headmaster, known to them all as the 'Old Man' or just 'OM', had to fight to keep them in Petersfield. An LCC inspector considered the organization of the school in the town to be completely inadequate and recommended transferring Emanuel to Basingstoke. Broom protested strongly. The school could not stand yet another upheaval. Parents would object, boys would be withdrawn, Basingstoke was a much less pleasant place. At Petersfield the boys were comfortable. 'This comfort', wrote Broom, 'is reflected in the general happiness of the boys who are now having their school life built up on normal lines. Football matches have been arranged, allotments taken over and concerts are being prepared. If boys are now suddenly moved, there will be amongst the younger boys at any rate a risk of difficult emotional and physical reactions to the change.' The LCC dropped its proposals and the school stayed in Petersfield.

The consensus by Christmas 1939, noted the school magazine, was that 'the essential vitality of the School has not been impaired'. Activities took place in the mornings, after a short service in the parish church. Lessons were squeezed in between 1.30pm and 5.30pm but boys were still being taught 30 periods a week. The dispersed nature of the temporary classrooms made

Drawing by Flora Twort of the statue of King William III in Market Square, Petersfield, from The Portcullis, *1941.*

Front gates of Churcher's College.

Men's Institute, the Methodist Sunday School, the Wesleyan Church Hall, the Town Hall, the Sun Inn and in a large hut behind the Blue Anchor Inn. It had also been intended for senior boys to attend Bedales, the small, co-educational experimental school nearby, but, to the dismay of the boys, this was restricted only to the sixth form biologists for two afternoons a week.

This influx must have had quite an impact on the town yet Emanuel enjoyed cordial relations with the people of Petersfield throughout the school's stay. This said a lot about the leadership of the Headmaster who took every opportunity to show the school's appreciation of its hosts. Before the end of 1939 the school had held a reception at the Red Lion for all those who had provided initial billets as well as a dinner dance for invited local guests. The school also organized public concerts and lectures. Emanuel tried as best it could to become a part of the town. Boys sang in a local production of *Messiah*, timetabling a nightmare but Aeron Rogers handled this with aplomb, keeping the show on the road by issuing a daily flurry of chits, distributed on bicycle by a pupil messenger to the form concerned. House activities were suspended only briefly, clubs and societies continued and for two nights each week boys met in the Methodist Hall to play games, read or write letters home. The OTC, under Charles Hill, was in its element, making the most of the acres of open space for operations, including night-time exercises. As for sport, most boys, thanks to the generosity of Churcher's College, had the chance to play team games almost as often as in London. Fixtures were inevitably curtailed but a combined team formed from Emanuel and Churcher's, known as the Hymnbooks (derived from Church-Manuels), took on visiting opposition and won.

Emanuel pupil in OTC uniform in Petersfield during the war.

But that first term in exile seemed unreal. 'Somehow', noted the school magazine, 'we felt we were living on a volcano which would erupt at any minute but the eruption never came'. In Petersfield war seemed distant. For many boys returning after Christmas, the contrast with gloomy London, with its shelters, sandbags and blackout, was marked. In one of the coldest of winters, Petersfield offered skating, tobogganing and skiing. There were several impromptu games of ice hockey with Churcher's College. Skating took place on Heath Pond and tobogganing on the slopes of the hill. Staff, including Mr Spafford, who was said to fall over better than anyone else, and Major Hill, who repeatedly said it was the first skating he had done since 1916, took to the ice as well.

Drawing of boys on OTC training around Petersfield, The Portcullis, *1942.*

Hill formed an OTC Skaters' Platoon which, it was reported, 'proceeded to carry out platoon and section drill at a great velocity'. An elderly local was heard to say, 'They be trainin' they troops for Finland.' There was plenty of snowballing but without much vigour – 'the general run of affairs was desultory snowballing of girls, who, so it seemed, liked it'.

The longer the war lasted, the more it impinged upon life in Petersfield. There was anxiety among the boys about the bombing raids on London. During 1940 daily routine was punctuated by frequent air raid warnings as a deadly game of cat and mouse took place in the summer skies over the town. In November 1940 boys from the corps were praised for their help in rescuing survivors from the debris of the property which received the only direct hit from a bomb suffered by the town during the war. Boys also helped in local rest centres as refugees from the heavy raids on Portsmouth filtered into the town. They provided a Home Guard Platoon which, one night in every eight, took turns to guard the tunnel on the London–Portsmouth railway line. The turmoil taking place in the world was very clear to sixth formers who sat their examinations in battle-dress, with their rifles and bayonets alongside. Soon all 17 year olds were required to serve in the Home Guard, the Auxiliary

OTC inspection at Petersfield during the Second World War.

Fire Service or Air Raid Precautions, while most of those over 16 took part in fire-watching duties. Several boys learned to drive tractors, a useful talent for the harvest camps organized during the summer vacations.

The list of Old Emanuel war dead grew longer. Deaths were announced of those who only months before had been in school, such as Derek Cadman, house prefect, sportsman, actor and corps sergeant, who had left at Christmas 1940, joined the RAF and was killed during training when his station was bombed in 1941. The OTC became the JTC (Junior Training Corps) and in 1942 carried out its first endurance march from Churcher's College to Emanuel in Wandsworth. Leaving at 11am on 31 March, the boys camped outside Guildford for the night and, having endured blisters, rain and hail, reached Emanuel the following evening. The exercise was repeated in the following year. In the autumn of 1941 boys were enthralled to have as their guests for several weeks five French schoolboys who had escaped from France to Britain by canoe, spending 30 hours at sea with limited rations. They left Emanuel to train with the Free French forces based in the UK.

The school was continually adapting to the constraints of wartime exile as a de facto boarding school. As staff were called up for war service, the first woman joined the staff, Mrs Canfield, wife of one of the departing masters. The Club, in the Methodist Hall, operating during the winter months, providing games, magazines, and 'really good film shows', proved very popular with senior boys. (Juniors were encouraged to remain in their billets during the blackout.) Groups of boys also enjoyed programmes of jazz, swing and classical music. Every effort was made to keep a range of other extra-curricular activities going, such as the Dorset Club, Photographic Society and Scientific Society. A Music Club was started and under Mr Crowther the Dramatic Society was revived, presenting an annual Christmas production in the Town Hall. Inter-school events were encouraged. There were debates with Portsmouth High School for Girls, Midhurst

THE BASE OF THE TOWER of Emanuel School, Wandsworth Common, hit by a bomb last month. The picture was released to-day.

The tower of Emanuel School was damaged by an enemy bomb on the night of 19 February, 1941.

Grammar School and Churcher's College. This fostered the creation of an inter-school sixth form discussion group, which also included pupils from Bedales and Petersfield Girls' High School. Allotments were started which produced sprouts, cabbages, broccoli and leeks. There were always problems to overcome in organizing sport, whether it was limited facilities or transport difficulties or timetable complications. Fencing was started for boys whose timetable commitments made team games difficult. Eventually boys were able to take up tennis, golf and fives. Inter-house swimming was made possible, once again thanks to the generosity of Churcher's College in sharing their pool. Rugby and cross-country matches, mainly away, took place against new opponents, such as Bryanston, Douai, Hurstpierpoint and Brighton College. Rowing was

Second World War memorial in the chapel commemorating Old Emanuels who gave their lives.

Lieutenant Michael H L McDonnell (1920–43), Royal Tank Regiment, died in North Africa. A member of Clyde House and a superb sportsman.

Flight Sergeant Douglas J Fitzgerald (1921–1944). Shot down in the same plane as another OE, Flight Sergeant Raymond C Fitzgerald (1921–1944).

Flight Sergeant Raymond C Fitzgerald (1922–1944). He had been married a few short weeks before he was killed.

Major Alan R J Skillern (1920–44), Royal Fusiliers, killed in Italy. His body was discovered by another OE, Major S C Warner MC, who said that Skillern was the greatest friend he ever had. He was school captain 1937, captain of rugby, captain of boats and a member of the shooting VIIIs.

Private Graeme Eric Richardson (1919–40), East Surrey Regiment. While at Emanuel he was Captain of Lyons and was remembered for his outgoing personality and beautiful singing voice.

Peter Harold Jackson (1920–43), Royal Armoured Corps, was awarded the Military Cross for his bravery early in the war.

Junior School pupils, Petersfield.

kept going but only on the Thames during school holidays, sometimes arousing the suspicion of the guards on Barnes Bridge who would demand to see the boys' identity cards.

Sustaining all these activities became more difficult as numbers began to decline at Petersfield and more families decided to keep their sons in London. This put the unity of the school under strain. With falling numbers at Petersfield – the roll fell from 450 to 350 between 1940 and 1942 – the house system, which had been struggling, was able to sustain only four houses, named Fiennes, Hampden, Dacre and Sackville. As more and more boys experienced nothing other than Emanuel at Petersfield, these names were intended to keep alive the memory of the school in Wandsworth. Many schools suffered from a breakdown in discipline and spirit during their wartime evacuation. Emanuel fared better than many, thanks not just to Cyril Broom and his staff but

also to the hospitality and co-operation the school enjoyed in Petersfield, particularly from Churcher's College. But telltale signs did surface. An editorial in the school magazine in the autumn of 1941 criticized the flippant attitude of senior boys towards school life and traditions, describing it as 'mental and physical apathy'. This was blamed on evacuation, which through safety from the war had provided only 'purposeless freedom'; and, paradoxically, while developing self-reliance and self-confidence, had made boys 'cocksure'. The magazine also ascribed this to a feeling of *carpe diem* in the face of service on the front line on leaving school. All this had led to 'the laxness of discipline, decline of ambition and lack of interest' in older boys, likely to lead to 'a deterioration in school standards'. The school should be seen as a rock of stability in uncertain times and 'we must not let everything slide'.

Cyril Broom's concern for the unity of the school grew as boys drifted back to London. The governors believed it was critical to re-establish a presence in Wandsworth but their request to open emergency classes there in 1940 had been rejected by the LCC. Instead, Emanuel boys began to attend the South-West London Emergency Secondary School for Boys. In the spring of 1943, as this school became crowded, it was the turn of

First XI cricket, Petersfield, 1941.

Scouts filling sandbags as part of the war effort, Petersfield.

the LCC to press the governors to permit classes to be opened at Emanuel, taking in not just Emanuel boys but also boys from Battersea Grammar School and Sir Walter St John's School. The governors were only too eager to oblige and classes were started under Charles Hill and Dr Newell, the music master. Mrs Broom, who had never enjoyed Petersfield, also returned to Wandsworth, keeping an eye on things for her husband. The oldest boys were under 15 but every effort was made to run the school normally. Drake, Howe, Marlborough and Wellington houses were revived and prefects appointed. Drama and music were encouraged and the Sackville Club re-formed. A corps was re-established, the range repaired and shooting restarted. Soccer was played during the winter but cricket during the summer of 1944 was interrupted by Hitler's flying bombs, which also halted the athletic sports. A flying bomb very nearly killed Mrs Broom when it hit the

A V1 flying over London.

A V1 propaganda leaflet dropped by German planes over southern England.

bus on which she was travelling. She was seriously injured but made a full recovery. Boys often spent night after night in their shelters, with as many as half absent at the start of school on a morning. When sirens sounded during the day, two senior boys were posted with helmets and whistles, ready to signal when a V1 bomb was approaching. The bell was rung as well as whistles sounded, the signal for boys to move to the shelters (the brick-windowed cloakrooms and changing-room). Although these breaks were often no more than a few minutes, they were frequent enough to cause considerable disruption to teaching. The devastation caused by these bombs was so extensive that they also brought to a halt all the repair work on the school buildings outstanding from 1941 so that scarce labour could be directed to higher priorities. But the Wandsworth tutorial classes proved their worth, attracting boys to the school who would otherwise have gone elsewhere and re-kindling the old traditions, creating a firm base on which the school could rebuild once peace returned. By the end of the war, there were 249 Emanuel boys at Wandsworth, compared with 229 in Petersfield.

In the spring of 1944 rumours abounded in Petersfield that a return to London was imminent. These multiplied as D-Day got under way. As tanks passed through Petersfield to the coast, one boy, Ron Williamson, from the first-floor window of his billet, was able to hand out tea to the tank crews. But D-Day came and went and still the school remained in Petersfield. Academically, the school had done as well as could be expected in the circumstances, notching up 37 scholarships, 284 School Certificates, 87 Higher School Certificates and 30 university wartime short course places. But with shrinking numbers, and the lowest number entered for the School Certificate in 1945 since 1920, the Headmaster believed another year would do grave damage to the school. The house system had to be

suspended and the staff, already weakened by call-ups and retirements, was further reduced by the transfer of masters to London. It was also more and more difficult to find suitable or willing billets for boys as the war ground on so two hostels, catering for 50 boys, were opened, one run by Mearns with his sister, Mrs Johnston, as matron, and later Mr Hipkins; while the second, used only in the last year of evacuation, was in the charge of Mr and Mrs Hyde.

Teachers at Emanuel in Wandsworth shortly after hearing that the war had been won.

It was only on 20 July 1945, almost three months after VE Day and five days before the end of the summer term, that Emanuel School left Petersfield. On a hot, sunny day a large number of residents gathered at the station to see the boys depart by special train while Churcher's College JTC paraded with their band to say farewell. Peter Pinkham recalled how the boys left Petersfield and arrived back in Wandsworth:

Boys were hanging out of every window of the packed train waving and yelling excitedly at the crowds on the platform, who were no doubt glad to see the last of us. My first sight of Emanuel School left me with a sense of foreboding. A Victorian pile, its walls were blackened with soot from countless trains passing by. Inside, the school exhibited an air of cold, cheerless neglect. As returning evacuees, we looked suitably tired and grey, with dark circles under the eyes, the result of having lived through six exhausting years of war.

No doubt Cyril Broom shared the same foreboding. He must have been a man of great resilience and resourcefulness. He had spent a decade before the war picking up the pieces left by his predecessor and knocking the school into reasonable shape. He had fought throughout the war years to keep the school together. He was now returning to buildings which were in an even worse state than he had left them, with a school of two halves he had to forge into one.

MAIN PICTURE: *The Headmaster, Cyril Broom, and Emanuel pupils celebrating VE Day in Petersfield, May 1945. Many of the pupils had already returned to London by the end of the war.*
INSET: *Emanuel pupils in Petersfield, 1944.*

Prefects, 1945.

He was also in charge of a school which had changed its status. Under the 1944 Education Act Emanuel became a voluntary aided school. Emanuel, as a school grant-aided by the local authority, did not have the option of direct grant status nor was it financially strong enough to opt for independence. Another consequence of the Act for the school was that as fees could no longer be charged, the Junior School, which had enjoyed so much success, closed in 1949. The Minister of Education, R A Butler, the man behind the Act, was the school's guest of honour at its 350th anniversary celebrations on 14 May 1945, postponed from 6 June the previous year, which had happened to be D-Day. The Lord Mayor and Viscount Hampden were also in attendance at the lunch at the Dorchester which followed the service in St Margaret's, Westminster. Butler said he came to reassure the school about its future. He valued a varied contribution from schools so essential for the future of the education but he begged the school never to forget quality. 'If you let go quality, you will go down. Maintain it and you will have a great future before you.' The Head spoke of the success of the school in holding together in

evacuation, of his hope that the school would continue to find freedom and independence under the new Act, and of his wish for a modern-day benefactor to rebuild the school. The governors made every effort to ensure they retained as much authority as possible under the Act and that scope for the LCC to interfere in the daily running of the school was as limited as possible. It soon became clear that the relationship between the two parties would not be easy. Only ten days after the school had been reunited in Wandsworth, the LCC proposed an abortive scheme to group Emanuel with two other local schools.

The Head's wish for a benefactor was deeply felt. He complained in public at Speech Day in 1946 that the top floor could not be occupied, the heating system was in disrepair, the chapel and old gym badly needed refurbishing and the playing field was unfit for use. One improvement much appreciated by subsequent generations was the extensive tree-planting scheme along the drive and around the grounds supervised by Stafford Hipkins in the same year. Unfortunately the only benefactor in sight was the LCC which offered under its London Development Plan in 1947 to rebuild Emanuel as a four-form entry school for 650 boys at an estimated cost of £117,000, the equivalent of more than £3 million today. But the Head and governors were suspicious of the

Ernest Bevin, Labour politician and statesman, giving out awards at prize giving, 1947.

A service for the school's 350th anniversary was held at St Margaret's, Westminster in 1945 (a year late due to the war). Distinguished guests included R A Butler, the Minister of Education, the Lord Mayor of London and Viscount Hampden.

LCC's motives – which would probably have removed ownership of the new buildings from the UWF – and dug in their heels, pressing for completion of the pre-war building programme. Even the offer by the LCC to demolish and rebuild only part of the buildings met with opposition. As a result, in the straitened economic times of post-war austerity, when building controls were still in force, Emanuel would have no new buildings until 1957.

Yet apart from the perennial problem of the buildings, and the poor examination results of the immediate post-war years, blamed on wartime conditions, Broom achieved unity and stability remarkably quickly. He soon established sound standards of discipline within the school although he lamented what he saw as a post-war breakdown in moral standards and how 'the ordinary human boy with a nonchalance that endeared, whilst it infuriated, remained serenely careless about the loss of property, litter or damage'. These were minor transgressions and there was nothing much more serious than boys smoking at the top of the tower. Sporting activities got under way on borrowed pitches, while clubs, societies and the Parents' Association were revived, drama

The Lord Mayor, Sir Denys C F Lowson, inspecting the CCF guard of honour outside the Guildhall in 1951 during the 350th anniversary celebrations of the granting of the school's charter by Queen Elizabeth I.

blossomed, open days were organized, overseas visits and French and German exchange trips reappeared, and the prefects' dances featured once more in the school calendar.

When inspectors visited the school towards the end of 1947, they pinpointed one reason for this rapid turnaround. Broom, they said, 'has good organizing ability and – what is far more important – high intellectual and social standards, and these standards are reflected in his choice of staff'. It was this which perhaps would be Broom's most valuable contribution to the school. While many staff left the school for promotion, itself a sign of Broom's good judgement, they were replaced by others of equal calibre, often charismatic individuals returning to peacetime careers after distinguished war service. The inspection report regarded Emanuel staff as very well qualified, noting that 'indeed, some of the masters are men of unusual culture and intellectual standards'. Many of them were 'exceptionally good teachers' who set high academic and social standards for the boys which was evident from their friendliness and confidence. Typical of Broom's new appointments were young men like T E Graham, John Brown, Stanley Inward and Paul Craddock. Graham, who was behind the revival in the school's drama, was appointed in 1946, an able teacher of French, inspiring a succession of scholars. Brown, who taught English, was, one former pupil later recalled, 'the enthusiast personified', once teaching a form of sixth formers suffering from chicken pox from his car outside the window of their first-floor classroom. Inward joined in 1947 to teach biology. A quiet and astute man, his pupils would include a future Zoological Society gold medallist, a future professor of genetics and an eminent mycologist. Craddock, a bear of a man, came to Emanuel in 1949 after wartime service in the Intelligence Corps. Nicknamed 'Joe' after 'Uncle Joe' Stalin for his fervently held socialist beliefs, he was an inspirational teacher of German and

Cover of Guildhall programme. 683 boys took part in the celebration.

Emanuel School

POUR · BIEN · DESIRER

Celebration of 350th Anniversary of Grant of Charter of Incorporation to Emanuel Hospital by Queen Elizabeth

On the 22nd October, 1951, at 2.30 p.m. in Guildhall

In 1951 the school celebrated the 350th anniversary of the granting of its royal charter with a visit from Queen Elizabeth. CLOCKWISE FROM TOP LEFT: *Queen Elizabeth, later the Queen Mother, receiving a bouquet of flowers; boys preparing to photograph the Queen; planting the magnolia tree which now stands in the South Courtyard.*

later reintroduced Russian to the curriculum. He was able to converse in languages as diverse as French and Italian, Czech, Serbo-Croat and Finnish. He was also an enthusiastic sportsman, coaching the first XI at cricket for many years. Another of Broom's appointments was the Reverend M M Griffiths as chaplain in 1951. During the 11 years he was at Emanuel, he revived the chapel as a focal point of the school, with regular services of holy communion, annual confirmation classes and the institution of the service of Carols and Nine Lessons in the Christmas term. For Broom, a Christian ethic was a steadfast constant in a quickly changing post-war world.

As Broom neared retirement, Emanuel was once again, as it had been in the late 1930s, a school parents wanted their sons to attend. By the start of his last year, in October 1952, there were 731 boys at the school. During the previous year Emanuel had celebrated the 350th anniversary of the school's charter. The Archbishop of Canterbury presented the prizes and Queen Elizabeth visited the school, planting a magnolia tree to mark the event. Broom had always valued the history and traditions of the school so it was appropriate he should still be in charge. But he was never complacent. At Speech Day in 1948 he had stressed that the school 'must be ready to adapt itself to change, though he hoped this could be

Emanuel first VIII boats club with Michael Aspel, two from left on back row, and Colonel Hill next to him, 1949.

Admission ticket for the Queen's visit.

EMANUEL SCHOOL

———

Visit of
HER MAJESTY THE QUEEN

Wednesday, November 7th, 1951

———

This ticket must be shown at the gates between
2 and 2.45 p.m. in order to secure admission

achieved without sacrificing its independence'. In his last Speech Day address in 1953, pointing to the growing realization of the services and major companies that grammar school boys would make excellent leaders of industry or commissioned officers, he spurned the label 'academic' when applied to grammar schools for he believed that they turned out boys of much broader horizons, being 'important nurseries of men with the capacity to improve human relations in the outside world'. He believed the school was in a sound state, adding prophetically that 'nothing but a revolution would affect its individuality or curb its full development along its chosen lines'. A later writer said of Broom, that 'though perhaps a little grave and detached and even slightly Olympian, he was greatly respected. He was sound, hardworking, consistent and shrewd'. One former pupil, Michael Aspel, later recollected a softer side to his Headmaster, describing him as 'an endearing, popular and perfect example of the owl-like academic with a twinkle in the eye'. On Broom's departure, the school magazine, highlighting his achievements, including 85 Oxbridge open scholarships over 25 years, emphasized in particular 'the high standard of personal behaviour which he has inculcated in the boys and on which ultimately the school's reputation rests'. He had made an outstanding contribution to the school.

6

1953–1975
The Return to
Independence

BROOM'S SUCCESSOR WAS THE FIRST former pupil to become Headmaster. John Brownson Clowes Grundy, born in Wandsworth in 1902, was also the oldest man to be appointed. Known as Jack, he had been head boy, captain of rugby, boats and boxing at Emanuel where he had followed his two elder brothers. They were both killed during the First World War, a blow from which Grundy never really recovered. He was plagued for the rest of his life by an irrational sense of guilt that he had been too young to serve before the war ended. He won an Exhibition to Fitzwilliam College, Cambridge, where he read modern languages, followed by a doctorate at University College, London. He had spent his career alternating between teaching in England and teaching and working overseas. In England he taught at St Paul's, Shrewsbury and Harrow, where he was senior modern languages master. Overseas he taught English at Gottingen University, became the first representative of the British Council in Helsinki and headed the British Institute in Cairo. He did serve during the Second World War, taking part in the Normandy landings.

Metalwork class, 1950s.

John Brownson Clowes Grundy, Headmaster 1953–63 and an alumnus of the school.

In many ways Emanuel flourished during the decade he was Head. Grundy, like Broom, was elected to the HMC, an achievement not open to his successor after HMC limited membership to fee-paying schools. Emanuel built on the academic reputation established through the staff appointed by Broom. Pupils such as Claude Scott, Ray Grainger, Mike Markland and Vic Dodds believed masters such as Craddock and Rogers drew out the potential of the most able boys. They described many of the staff as 'really mature men of the world', derived from wartime service. They were

idiosyncratic, charismatic and strongly individualistic, often deliberately cultivating their eccentricities for the edification of their pupils. While those appointed by Broom were coming into their own, staff from an earlier generation, such as Hipkins, Hirst and Hyde, were reaching retirement. In their place Grundy recruited teachers such as J A Cuddon, K W Ulyatt and Derek Pennell.

Cuddon, known either as Jack, after his initials, or Charles, came to the school in 1954 and spent 39 years at Emanuel as an inspired teacher of English. A prolific writer in almost any form, whether novels, plays, essays or poetry, he wrote one of the best travel books in English, *The Owl's Watchsong*, and became well known for *A Dictionary of Sport and Games* and his *Dictionary of Literary Theory*. He turned to teaching because it gave him the time to write and, as one pupil, Steve Gooch, put it, 'however promptly you raced away from your last class, Mr Cuddon could always be seen, off in the distance, racing still faster'. When Peter Hendry was asked to describe Cuddon, he remarked that '"laid back" had not been invented then but he certainly reclined'. He was a man whom the current generation would probably call 'cool'. Yet in the classroom he was almost always brilliant, clad in his shabby jackets and lost in a fog of cigarette smoke. One boy, Henry King, whose strength lay in science, was studying English only as a sixth form option but found Cuddon 'instilled in me, a doomed would-be scientist, a love of Chesterton, Pope, Spenser, Zola, Waugh and Anthony Powell'.

Dr Kenneth Ulyatt came as master in charge of the growing sixth form in 1955 and later became head of science. Absent-minded, austere but urbane, described by one pupil as 'Corinthian', with a habit of lying on the bench in front of the class, he was a teacher of the old school but one who taught with clarity and had an outstanding success with the lower physics set in the sixth form. Derek Pennell was another scientist, appointed immediately after graduation in 1960, who also became head of science. Known as 'Daffy' after his initials (DAFP), his pupils would include a string of Oxbridge scholars, among them Tim Berners-Lee.

The common room remained an almost entirely male preserve, but there was one woman in the school just as strong as her male counterparts. Mary Davies joined Emanuel in 1954 as school secretary and secretary to the Headmaster, retaining the latter post until her retirement in 1995. A history graduate, she was discreet, loyal and utterly supportive of all the Heads for whom she worked. Jack Grundy later described her as 'a pearl beyond price'.

With a volcanic but short-lived temper, she was held in awe by many staff, astonishing the common room by invading this male space to eat her sandwiches every lunchtime.

The congeniality of the common room was appreciated by many new staff. Christian Strover, who joined the music department in 1956, described it as civilized, refined, courteous and friendly; Peter Hendry, who came to Emanuel in 1959, found it welcoming and cheerful with a strong sense of unity and a deep commitment to the school. These two qualities would prove invaluable in the difficult years to come, as both the leadership of the school and its future in the hands of the LCC and its successors came into question.

The calibre of staff was one reason for the school's excellent academic results. The other was the consequence of the 1944 Education Act and the change in the school's status. Through the eleven-plus system, Emanuel was automatically being sent many of the most able boys leaving the local LCC primary schools. Between 1953 and 1959 Emanuel boys won 25 open university awards and 29 state scholarships. Without these awards, it was often impossible for boys from less well-off backgrounds to afford university. By 1959 a quarter of all leavers from Emanuel were taking up university places. Emanuel's sixth form flourished, rising from just 60 boys in 1947 to almost 200 by 1960. The sixth form curriculum was ahead of its time in permitting combinations such as maths with foreign languages, while options allowed boys to study non-examination subjects. The report of the 1959 inspection noted that 'boys of the highest ability can reach the standards of

which they are capable, such is the academic calibre and teaching power of the staff responsible for sixth form work; indeed scholarship work is sometimes better than Advanced level work'.

The report continued that 'the more ordinary Sixth Former is also well provided for' but it was more critical of the performance of boys at 'O' level. Improvement would come, said the report, only 'as closer attention is given to the needs of the slower pupil'. For some boys, Emanuel was an academic treadmill. They had little idea of what they were aiming for, with some staff making sweeping assumptions about their academic potential. The quieter, shyer, less academic boys could find this daunting although they had their saviours among the staff. One was Ron Tovey, the woodwork teacher. Although he pretended that first years were scarcely worth his while teaching, his warm manner in a department away from the main school did much to encourage the less confident. The performance of less able boys at 'O' level was clearly a problem at Emanuel although the Headmaster apparently believed it had been remedied by 1962. He noted at Speech Day that year 'the steady rise of the bottom Fourth and Fifth forms from their original function of academic "dustbins" to their present status as very worthy units of the School'. His language rather betrayed the school's previous attitude but it was not unusual in many academic schools of the time. In Grundy's last year, 1963, the pass rate at 'O' level was 72 per cent and at 'A' level 77 per cent, although there were only 52 'A' grades at 'A' level from 87 candidates taking 245 subjects.

Nevertheless, as the inspectors had pointed out, such results still made Emanuel 'one of the leading grammar schools of London'.

Throughout the 1950s there were between 750 and 800 boys at the school. In the early 1960s more than half of them lived within two miles of the school, coming from a mix of working-class and middle-class backgrounds, although a rising minority was travelling in from

Surrey every day. In general the boys were friendly, lively and responsive, although the decrepit quality of the school buildings, and the cold, unadorned interior, tended to amplify their natural boisterousness. The buildings remained noisy, crowded, shabby and depressing, with peeling paintwork and ill-fitting doors. For the swimming bath and changing rooms, the old assembly hall, the outside lavatory block and the fives court, the inspectors could only find the word 'squalid'. Hopes in the early 1950s that the LCC might fund a major building programme were in vain. There was a justified suspicion that the LCC, in allocating funding for new buildings, was prejudiced against the grammar schools in general, and against Emanuel in particular. Jack Grundy was antipathetic towards the authority and pursued a policy of having as little to do with the LCC as possible. But the governors too could seem indifferent. The school was often cold and during the severe winter of 1962–3 it was so cold that, Christian Strover recalled, 'the governors were called in and taken on a tour of the top floor where pupils were working in overcoats, gloves and scarves. Their only comment was that it was "very healthy"'.

There was some progress. The school gates, missing since being taken away for scrap during the war, were replaced with a smaller pair in 1954. Lord Exeter opened a new workshop on the site of the old gym, comprising wood and metal shops, drawing and printing rooms, in February 1957. A month earlier arson had destroyed the Hampden Hall, the culmination of a series of fires and hoax alarms during the late 1950s. Viscount Hampden opened a replacement, seating 100 more boys than its predecessor, in October 1959. The War Memorial Fund was dedicated to a new pavilion, opened on 19 July 1958 by Cyril Broom. A scheme to erect a new boathouse at Barnes Bridge was completed in 1959 thanks to a generous donation by the Wates brothers, directors of the family construction business, all of whom had attended the school. The kitchens were remodelled, with new equipment and the provision of a masters' dining room, in 1960. Two years later existing accommodation was turned into art rooms and a new common room. In the summer of 1963 new fives courts were opened and a new rowing tank was installed.

The severity of the buildings was matched by the severity of the discipline. Corporal punishment, by cane

The remains of the Hampden Hall after the disastrous fire of 1957. The current hall dates from 1958.

Staff photo, 1964. Front row: Mary Davies (secretary), Tommy Thompson, Paul Craddock, Dennis Witcombe, Bernard Slater, Harry Mearns, Charles Hill, Stafford Hipkins, Claude Neath, Aeron Rogers, Tom Graham, Christian Strover, Peter Hendry (head of English – later Headmaster), Stan Inward. Middle row: Kenneth Ullyatt, Graeme Willison, A N Other, Geoffrey Armstead (chaplain), Mr Tasker, Philip Cooper, Eddie Casale, Charles Cuddon, Roger Chignell, David Englebach, A N Other, John Lawrence, Derek Pennell, Dick Raine, Harry Rodwell, John Hammond, John Richardson. Back row: B Read, Derek Drury, Mr Jefferies, Colin MacFarquhar, Mr Whitehall, Peter Jones, John Ashwin, Arnold Cruise, Francis Grundy, A N Other, A N Other, Guy Nelder, John Manning, Ron Tovey.

or slipper, was widespread, exercised by the Head, the staff and the prefects. Although it was described by one master as just 'part of the routine', the surviving punishment book records 208 canings between 2 November 1962 and 15 July 1963. Of these, sixth formers, several of them upper sixth formers, received 33 canings. Offences ranged from cutting exam revision and a bad report to bullying, cheating, smoking, exceeding bounds, lateness and poor work. Six of the best were most often given for accumulating three hours' detention. Sometimes the severity of the caning exceeded reasonable bounds. Edgar Asher, who left the school in 1956, recalled how a few staff 'were brutal in their discipline and exhibited violent traits that would be totally unacceptable today'. Beatings were usually handed out in the dreaded room 19, the masters' bathroom, on a Friday lunchtime. Matters came to a head when one sixth former, who had caused a disturbance in assembly and refused to be beaten on the grounds that the punishment was out of all proportion to the offence, was subsequently expelled. The issue came before the governors and also reached the Ministry of Education, which agreed with the boy and his parents, insisting the expulsion be deleted from his school record. The governors were obviously concerned and, in the knowledge that a number of boys had not only been expelled in recent years but had also been withdrawn by their parents, asked for a list of them from the Head. The long-serving chairman of governors, R C E Austin, made plain to the Head his dismay that boys of 17 and 18 were being caned. He insisted that in such cases corporal punishment should only be used as a last resort and 'not indulged in frequently'. The matter found its way into the press and did no favours to the school.

Grundy was a complex figure, inspiring respect and contempt in equal measure among those who knew him. In 1987 his obituarist in the school magazine noted that there were hundreds of different opinions about him. Some thought him 'stubborn, arrogant, ill-tempered, tactless and inconsistent', while others considered him 'sane, far-sighted, efficient, firm and kindly'. His relationship with the common room was difficult throughout his period in office. One member of staff, appointed by the Head, described him as pleasant and affable, insistent on high academic standards, but impulsive and autocratic. Opinions about Grundy among the boys were equally polarized. Some boys believed he was a man who set high standards, who did his best to see they were upheld and who helped to instil a sense of tradition. Others saw him as a bully, rigidly Edwardian in his outlook, a man out of his times. Grundy appeared impervious to all the tension around him. He always seemed to display, wrote J A Cuddon, a 'jaunty insouciance when faced with adversity'. The chapter relating to the school in his bland autobiography,

published after his retirement, was titled 'Ten Harmonious Years'. When Cuddon suggested this was a travesty of the truth, Grundy's response was, 'but, to me, they were harmonious'.

Aside from academic standards, rowing and the corps were Grundy's particular interests. The CCF still played a central role in the school, remaining under the command of Charles Hill until his retirement after 30 years in 1961. The great majority of boys were members. It was seen as a route to becoming a prefect and, in the days of National Service, it also helped boys to win commissions. Grundy also did much to develop rowing. He realized the temporary premises used by the boat club were totally unsatisfactory and was behind the appeal to raise funds for the new boathouse completed through the generosity of the Wates brothers. He also brought Derek Drury from Chiswick Grammar School to Emanuel in 1955. Drury transformed the sport. Under him, rowing

THIS AND FACING PAGE (MAIN PICTURE): *The CCF in action in the late 1950s.*

TOP, MIDDLE AND RIGHT: *In the 1950s the Grasshopper II, a primary sail-plane, was catapult launched on the Field so that the RAF section of the CCF could acquire the elements of practical airmanship.*

superseded rugby as the sport of first choice at the school. One boy recalled how Drury introduced the new 'spoon' blades at Emanuel which became the first school to use them in the local regattas. A hard taskmaster but greatly respected, he transformed the attitude and skills of those boys who rowed. A new eight was bought, the boys were permitted, in return for training early on the river, to miss assembly and the result that year was second place in the Schools Head of the River. This was so unexpected that the crew as usual went off to a local cafe for tea and missed the presentation. In 1960 Emanuel won the Public Schools Challenge Cup at the Kingston regatta after a gap of nearly 40 years. Two years later, the school achieved its first victory in the Schools Head, repeating the feat in the following year, and rowed for the first time in the Princess Elizabeth Cup at the Henley regatta. But the greatest achievement was yet to come.

Other than rowing, perhaps the most noteworthy performance of the school during the Grundy years was the cricketing achievement of Vic Dodds, who set a new school batting record, scoring 124 not out against Alleyns in 1963, under the coaching of Paul Craddock. Clubs and other activities continued much as ever, with minor

protests against the Head's renaming of the Dacre Club as the Dacre Society, regarded as sacrilege. The boys could not remember, of course, as Grundy did, that the latter had been its original name. Although drama tended to be neglected, music had more attention than it had enjoyed since the days of 'Bandy' Evans. The school's strength lay in choral work, fostered initially by Bernard Oram, although his notorious reputation as a feared disciplinarian detracted from any joy there may have been in performing. This was restored under the two music masters who replaced him in the mid-1950s, Donald Cashmore and Christian Strover. In 1959 the trebles and altos from Emanuel's concert choir joined the chorus at the Royal Albert Hall for a performance of Mahler's Eighth Symphony under Jascha Horenstein. After Benjamin Britten visited the school a year later, the choir was invited both to perform in a concert of his Spring Symphony and to take part in the subsequent recording. When Cashmore left in 1961, Strover remained. Until his retirement in 1998, he made it his task to bring as much variety as possible to Emanuel's musical life, often at times when music did not enjoy a high priority within the school.

BOAT CLUB   Tel: 020 8870 8136

MAIN PICTURE: *The school's boathouse at Barnes first opened in 1959 and remains a key fixture in the life of the school today.* FAR LEFT: *Training on the River Thames in front of the boathouse.* LEFT: *Derek Drury, the rowing coach who oversaw many of Emanuel's greatest rowing triumphs.* BELOW: *Lifting a new eight into the river.*

A window featuring the Chelsea arms designed by Moira Forsyth.

think of the school as it had been when he was a boy, was absolute and the real influence on the school was the LCC and its successor, the Inner London Education Authority (ILEA), which paid to keep the school going. Grundy never relished the relationship with local government which was becoming more and more intrusive. The governors expected the Head to serve until 1967 but he decided unexpectedly to leave at Christmas 1963. He always cited the looming reorganization of London schools as his reason for going although, after the events relating to discipline earlier in the year, he may have understood the limitations of his style of headship. He left for a senior teaching post abroad at Fourah Bay College in Sierra Leone. He had certainly furthered the school's academic reputation but sometimes the manner in which he had done so had been unfortunate, in particular the way discipline had been administered and the rift which had opened up with the common room.

The era of his successor, Charles Kuper, was increasingly dominated by ILEA's plans for the reorganization of London's schools. This brought out the best in Emanuel's staff whose key role in the campaign to retain grammar-school status and then to seek independence

The chapel remained central to school life. The windows shattered during the war were replaced with stained glass featuring graceful and elegant designs by Moira Forsyth, dedicated respectively by the Bishop of Southwark in 1954 and the Bishop of Kingston in 1955. As many as 90 boys were attending monthly communion in the mid-1950s, around 40 were confirmed each year, and by the end of the decade, thanks to the generosity of Norman Wates, the choir were appearing in robes and cassocks for the first time since the 1930s. Grundy revived ancient links with the parish of Chelsea. A stained-glass panel with the Chelsea arms was installed in 1961 and the Vicar of Chelsea invited the Emanuel choir to sing annually in the Old Church.

Although the Emanuel governors, under Frank Abbott, had become a governing body in their own right in 1957, rather than a committee of the UWF, they were often as distant from the school as ever. Meetings were short, the authority of the chairman, who was inclined to

Moira Forsyth at work in her studio. Forsyth was commissioned to design new stained glass for the chapel to replace the glass that had been shattered in the war.

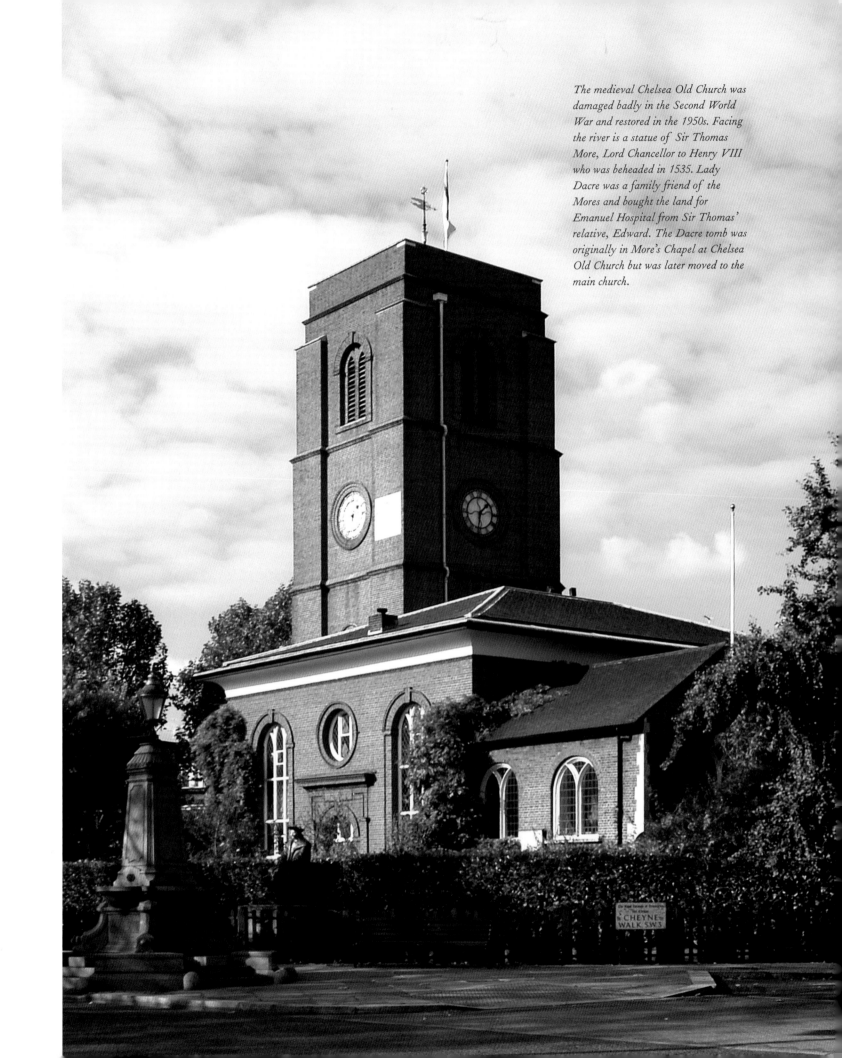

The medieval Chelsea Old Church was damaged badly in the Second World War and restored in the 1950s. Facing the river is a statue of Sir Thomas More, Lord Chancellor to Henry VIII who was beheaded in 1535. Lady Dacre was a family friend of the Mores and bought the land for Emanuel Hospital from Sir Thomas' relative, Edward. The Dacre tomb was originally in More's Chapel at Chelsea Old Church but was later moved to the main church.

demonstrated the strength of their loyalty and commitment. But this also highlighted the gap between the energy they invested in this fight and the limited leadership given by the Head.

Kuper was a good man full of good intentions. He had a degree from Wadham College, Oxford, was one of the few volunteer reserve offices to command a Royal Navy ship during the war and came to Emanuel having been Headmaster of Queen Mary's School, Basingstoke. Warm, relaxed and friendly, described by one member of staff as 'toffee-hearted', he was kindly and forgiving in private while traditionally stern in public. This contrast was seen in his approach to discipline. He was horrified by the way in which the school dealt with errant sixth formers. In future, such discipline would be handled by the Headmaster alone, which, he hoped, would 'foster a greater sense of personal responsibility' among senior boys. Corporal punishment in general was greatly reduced under Kuper although he successfully urged the governors in 1974 not to follow ILEA's example in banning the practice, which he believed would have an adverse effect on school discipline. In place of the widespread use of the cane, Kuper introduced the much more effective conduct card system.

Charles Kuper, Headmaster 1964–75.

But Kuper, like his predecessor, was not a forward-looking Headmaster. He looked back to the grammar-school tradition of the 1930s and was perplexed by the social changes of the 1960s. A bachelor, who lived with his sister and mother, he was also ill when he arrived at Emanuel (his alcoholism was not detected because he was appointed without a medical examination). His health deteriorated under the pressures of the post and the isolation of his position, symbolized by the loneliness of the Headmaster's house in a part of London which was beginning to seem run-down. He had the interests of the school at heart but found it difficult to translate his innate understanding of boys into practical management or effective control. His military inclinations became more and more pronounced, not to say eccentric, particularly in his use of the school's tannoy system. Lessons were increasingly interrupted by his messages, usually beginning, 'Do you hear there?' He relied heavily on his second masters, notably Peter Hendry, as well as his secretary, Mary Davies, described by one former pupil as 'the administrative binding keeping the school together'.

The task confronting Kuper would have daunted a fitter man. He came to the school in the year when a Labour government was elected which was committed to

Snapshots from school life, mostly taken by Roger Clarke in the early 1960s. Facing page, main picture: *Watching the trains on a school trip.* Below, from left: *The chemistry laboratory; The tuck shop; Mr and Mrs Cakebread presiding over the tuck shop; John Williams – notable for playing for the England rugby under 19s; Group of boys; The cricket nets; Denis Witcombe and family, Dacre Day 1963.*

Walking up the drive to school.

was formed. The sticking point between ILEA and Emanuel was the insistence of the former on removing the selection of pupils by ability. There was an absolute resistance on this point from almost everyone concerned with the school, whose aim was to secure Emanuel's future as a grammar school. ILEA's initial plans, unveiled in the summer of 1966, proposed the amalgamation of Emanuel with Spencer Park, the adjacent, newly created comprehensive school. There was no support for this among either governors or parents who voted in meetings that autumn in favour of the status quo. Many parents also indicated a willingness to pay fees if independence was adopted. The governing body had already decided that this was the only option available if ILEA's proposals proved unacceptable.

Although ILEA dropped this idea, life became increasingly difficult for the school. Peter Hendry, who became second master in 1965, recalled how the heavily criticized 'eleven-plus' selective examination had been replaced that year by an ineffective pupil profile. The very vague ability banding made it almost impossible to make proper selections, aggravated by a decline in the number of applicants. This trend was already in evidence when Kuper arrived and there were, for instance, just 130 boys for 107 places in 1968. Uncertainty over the leadership of school as well as its future was producing lacklustre examination results. By the late 1960s the pass rate for 'A' and 'O' levels respectively was 69 per cent and 49 per cent. There had previously been some great individual triumphs, such as Peter Goddard, later Master of St John's, Cambridge, and there were also more to come, notably Tim Berners-Lee, the founder of the World Wide Web, who was at the school in the late 1960s and early 1970s. But these were no longer being achieved in the same numbers – there were 19 Oxbridge places for Emanuel boys in 1964 but only two in 1968 and eight in 1971. It was clear that too many pupils at Emanuel were failing to reach the same heights. By the early 1970s staff were even advising the father of one able boy to send his son elsewhere for 'A' levels while a former pupil recalled how most boys were not expected to enter university. There was perhaps too much inconsistency in the teaching, which was carried by a core of very capable teachers, including a few who were truly brilliant.

the introduction of comprehensive schools throughout the country. Nowhere would the battle over this issue be fought more fiercely, or more venomously, than in London. The government's intentions were clearly stated in a circular, 10/65, issued in October 1965, instructing all local education authorities to prepare appropriate schemes. In the same year, with the replacement of the LCC by the Greater London Council (GLC), the Inner London Education Authority (ILEA)

With some doubt over the future of the school, the Head shrewdly squeezed as much money as he could for new buildings out of ILEA. He did have a good case, of course, since the LCC had largely neglected the school in terms of capital spending. In 1966 the UWF funded a new classroom block and in April 1970 a new sixth form block, called the Dacre Block, funded by public money, was opened by the Lord Mayor of London, another link with the school's historic past. Kuper was also responsible for creating the much-needed new common room, freeing the old one for use as music rooms, and a new swimming pool. A major asset, the pool was opened in 1973 by Mrs Christine Abbott, wife of former pupil Frank Abbott, who had been chairman of governors since 1963. It was only completed two years later, however, when a roof was added. The entire cost had been raised through an appeal to parents, former pupils and friends of the school.

The new pool would help to strengthen swimming at a school which, while resting somewhat on its academic laurels, was still lauded for its sporting reputation. There were trophy successes in tennis, with the school winning the Clarke Cup in 1965 and the Youll Cup in 1965 and 1966; in cricket, when the first XI won the Cricketers' Trophy in 1970; and in rugby sevens, with the school winning several competitions in the early 1970s. But the most outstanding achievement, one which rocked the sport and is still talked about more than four decades later, was Emanuel's 1966 victory in the Princess Elizabeth Challenge Cup at Henley. Open to crews from home and abroad, this remains the premier public schools rowing trophy. The Emanuel eight in that year was the finest team Derek Drury ever coached at the school. It was commonly regarded as the best school crew produced in the UK for more than 60 years, chalking up a series of impressive wins. A sign of the team's quality came in the Open Head of the River when Emanuel finished sixth, unheard of for a schoolboy crew. John Neale, the cox, recalled how the crew enjoyed their rowing so much, they felt little pressure, which, with the professional approach cultivated by their coach, rival crews found disturbing. A hiccough occurred during the National Schools Championship at Pangbourne, when the team was disqualified for drifting into another lane.

Charles Kuper was waiting as the crew left the water. For him rowing represented a key part of the school's aspirations. Emanuel could not have a better ambassador to the outside world than the school rowing team. But he put his arm around Neale and reassured him that much worse things had happened. At Henley, there were jibes about the incident from the Radley crew, Emanuel's opposition in the semi-final, but this only strengthened the team's determination – Radley was crushed. Emanuel's boat had

Emanuel, pictured here about to overtake the crew in front, achieved the fastest time and won the Schools' Head of the River race for the first time in 1967. Since then Emanuel has won the Schools' Head of the River race 12 times – more times than any other school except Eton.

been delivered only three weeks before, thanks to John Cork, who had beaten the seamen's strike by driving all the way to Leghorn with a trailer on his car to bring the boat back. The makers, Doneratico, promised coach and crew a free holiday in the owner's 15th-century castle if they won the Princess Elizabeth Challenge Cup. The team had the crowd on their side as they rowed to victory over their much heavier rivals, the Halcyon Boat Club from St Paul's School in the US. It was the first time a British crew had beaten an American side in the final of the competition. The governors declared a whole holiday for the entire school and the team claimed their Italian holiday. Although the standard of rowing at Emanuel remained high under Drury's successor, P Jones, into the 1970s, there is no doubt that the side which achieved that famous victory in 1966 was the outstanding team of the era. Forty years later, on the anniversary of their triumph, they accepted a special invitation to row the course again.

By the early 1970s ILEA had revived its plans to reorganize the school. In 1972, when, coincidentally, the chairman of governors was serving as chairman of the GLC, another plan was proposed. This would turn Emanuel into a co-educational school, merging it with two girls' grammar schools, both significant distances

Celebrating one of the school's many rowing triumphs, 1968.

away. Like the previous plan, it was rejected as completely impractical. Two years later, with the election of a Labour government, ILEA redoubled its efforts. This time a different approach was adopted. No specific scheme was put forward but the school was told that if Emanuel continued to refuse to co-operate with ILEA over reorganization, then ILEA would stop maintaining the school. Independence was the only alternative, suggested ILEA's Education Officer, Dr Briault, but if this was the case he would prefer that it occurred as quietly as possible. But the many Emanuel staff who had committed the best years of their lives to the grammar school were not prepared to see its disappearance without a fight. Paul Craddock, a fervent socialist, took the lead in fighting the Labour authority. As chairman of the common room, he led an action committee which galvanized Emanuel into an exhausting campaign in defence of its grammar-school status. Public meetings were held, letters were written to the press, appearances were made on television and MPs were lobbied. Craddock, a master of language, was captivating in his eloquence. Other grammar schools, initially shy of joining the fray, followed Emanuel's lead. Emanuel also benefited from being part of the so-called Trinity Group, formed by the Headmaster of Trinity, Croydon, which

BELOW, LEFT: *Emanuel School Top Squad, 1966, winners of the Princess Elizabeth Challenge Cup at Henley and many other rowing trophies.* RIGHT: *The same crew was invited, 40 years later, to row past the Stewards Enclosure at Henley in recognition of the fact that their winning time in 1966 is still one of the fastest winning times ever achieved by an English crew in this event.*

A poster urging parents to join the fight to save Emanuel School from the designs of the local education authority.

brought together threatened direct-grant and voluntary-aided schools. Frank Abbott used his extensive influence within local government as best he could. Senior boys especially took a prominent part in the campaign. A relay team took a petition to Downing Street, the vests of the boys emblazoned with 'Save Emanuel School', and all the school eights rowed down the Thames to the Houses of Parliament. By the end of 1975, the opposition to ILEA's plans had provoked 241 letters of objection, containing nearly 3,000 signatures, and three petitions, one with more than 22,000 signatures. Yet still the Secretary of State for Education refused to receive a deputation from the school.

Emanuel suffered from the uncertainty over the school's future. Together with the illness of the Head, and the remoteness of the governing body from what was happening in the school, this created what one member of staff described as 'a great laxness'. Discipline declined, instances of corporal punishment crept up again,

Front cover of The Portcullis *showing the ILEA stamping on the school.*

although nowhere near the scale of the Grundy years, and absenteeism soared. The prominence of Emanuel's valiant fight against ILEA led pupils from Spencer Park, the neighbouring school, to target Emanuel boys. One Emanuel boy recalled how the CCF would mount evening patrols as a safeguard against vandalism. On his last day at school, the same pupil spied too late a boy on the perimeter of the school grounds raising an air rifle towards him. As he turned, a pellet pierced his school suit. The struggle also claimed the school's Headmaster. Charles Kuper gave notice in 1974 that he would retire a year later. Worn out, he said farewell to the school at the end of the summer term. He never saw retirement. He died at the school in early August.

Peter Hendry, the second master, took over as acting Head just as the fight over the school's future reached its climax. In February 1976, after the Secretary of State had confirmed ILEA's proposals, the governors formally resolved that the school

Peter Hendry, Headmaster 1975–84.

should become independent from the beginning of the autumn term. After relying on state aid for nearly a century, this was a daunting prospect. There was a crucial need, the governors believed, for continuity so in May they confirmed Peter Hendry as Headmaster. Educated at Colfe's, where Cyril Broom had been Head, and Keble College, Oxford, Hendry would have preferred to remain second master, where he felt he had more influence and which gave him more time for teaching. In his own words, he rather 'drifted into being a Headmaster'. But he had already shown qualities of leadership and professionalism, he was closely involved in the preparations for independence and he possessed a deep knowledge of the school's catchment areas. The first sign of the scale of the challenge he would face soon arrived. Without warning ILEA, having promised to fund 90 boys a year at the school after independence, cut the number to 60. At a time when recruitment was going to be difficult, this would make the school's task even harder.

School life from the 1970s. MAIN PICTURE: *Tennis on the grass court.*
SMALL PICTURES, FROM LEFT: *Staff – Craddock, Ogilvie, Cruise, Jack Town, Pennell, Kay (bottom left) and Basing; Christian Strover, director of music, taught at Emanuel for 40 years; Craddock, centre back, Peter Hendry, right, Derek Pennell, bottom right and Mike Kay, far left; Charles Hill (centre) with four former pupils who became teachers at Emanuel, Jack Town, Michael Stewart, Jerry Dale and Connor Mc Dermott.*

Production of Doctor Faustus, *with Jonathan Driver inspiring a young cast, 1994.*

1976–1994

A New Identity

THE STORY OF EMANUEL'S RETURN to independence can be divided into two parts. The first covers the difficult early years under Peter Hendry and his successor, Peter Thomson, when the challenges were to ensure the school survived, to adapt to independent status and to begin creating an identity for Emanuel as an independent school. The second shows how three different Heads, Tristam Jones-Parry, Anne-Marie Sutcliffe and Mark Hanley-Browne, built upon each other's contribution towards the development of a modernized, attractive, confident and fully co-educational school.

Coming to terms with independence was not easy. For the governors, Headmaster and staff, the most important thing left to Emanuel was its tradition and reputation. After so many people had invested so much time and energy in the fight to retain Emanuel's grammar-school status, and after the turbulence undergone by the school during the final years of Kuper's headship, it was understandable that everyone connected with the school should place so much importance on continuity. 'We tried', recalled Peter Hendry, 'to keep as much of the old feeling as possible.' Stability and continuity, certainly in the short term, were clearly desirable and achieving this was Peter Hendry's great contribution to Emanuel's future.

On the other hand, independence had fundamentally changed the school. Emanuel was free (albeit temporarily) from state interference but as a result it was short of money and could do little to improve the site and buildings which it owned. Nor could it any longer rely on a stream of scholarship boys directed to its doors by the local authorities. Its natural catchment area, Wandsworth and Battersea, was a part of London which was already experiencing urban decay. Above all, it was no longer a grammar school but an independent fee-paying boys' day school which now had to compete with many well-established similar schools throughout south London.

It was the change in status from grammar to independent school which presented the biggest challenge. Many believed that the school's past academic reputation would secure its future. Continuity, therefore, was essential. But the school could no longer expect the calibre of boys previously produced by the 'eleven-plus' system. As a result of the changes made to the system by ILEA in the late 1960s, there had already been some decline in standards. The school could sustain its reputation only if it had a sufficiently large pool of applicants from which to choose every year. As a result, one of the committees established to consider future admissions after independence concluded that standards could be maintained only if the number of pupils at Emanuel was reduced to between

THIS AND FACING PAGE: *School life from the late 1970s.* CLOCKWISE FROM LEFT: *The beginning of the school day; In the playground; Lunchtime in the dining room; Outside the tuck shop; Shooting practice.*

500 and 600. In any case it was estimated that numbers would fall to around 500 over ten years.

This was not an assessment the governors were happy to hear. For a cash-strapped school, it was essential that Emanuel was as full as possible. Until the school had established its place in the independent sector, it would be difficult for Emanuel to strike the right balance between keeping the school full and sustaining academic standards. Between the autumn of 1975 and the autumn of 1977, when fees were charged for the first time, numbers fell from 891 to 791. The situation became more acute as the last of the scholarship boys left the school. By 1979, when half the pupils were fee-payers, numbers had fallen further to 719. The governors, concerned that spending was outstripping income, pruned the budget to keep fees competitive with

Fête and Flannels Day in the 1990s.

local rivals. But as well as failing to attract pupils entering the school at 11, the sixth form was also shrinking as fifth formers chose to leave the school for sixth form colleges. The governors, noting the number of applicants being rejected, asked the Headmaster, 'without prejudice to the school's excellent academic record', to consider relaxing entry standards to boost numbers. Two decisions brought some relief to the crisis. Firstly, it was agreed to admit boys from the age of ten from September 1983. Princess Alexandra visited the school on 5 May 1983 to lay the foundation stone for the new junior classrooms. Secondly, the school took part in the Assisted Places Scheme devised by the Conservative government as a way of helping children from poorer families to attend independent schools. Emanuel seized the chance with relish, agreeing that it would take up to half of its annual intake as Assisted Places. It never reached that staggering level but did at its peak exceed 40 per cent, a proportion attained by few other schools. This harked back to the time when the school relied so heavily on LCC scholars. Assisted Places made all the difference. In November 1984, for instance, 185 of the 635 boys on the school roll were on Assisted Places. Without them, it is clear that Emanuel would have been in considerable trouble. But, as in the past, this lifeline came at a price. The

Princess Alexandra visited to lay the foundations for the new junior classrooms, 1983.

government controlled the fee levels for Assisted Places and they were not generous. For as long as Emanuel relied on Assisted Places, the school would continue to lack the resources to reinvigorate its ageing infrastructure.

Assisted Places brought some able boys to the school and also helped Emanuel to reflect the mixed racial composition of the local area. But Assisted Places could never make up for the loss of boys selected for the school from the most able of local primary school pupils. This change was difficult for staff, most of whom had never taught in anything other than grammar schools and many of whom had been at Emanuel for 20 years or more. Faced with pupils whose potential required more effort to develop, it was a challenge to adapt the way in which they taught. It was hardly surprising that this affected the school's academic reputation, earned during a period when its classrooms were filled only with 'eleven-plus' scholars.

In the summer of 1983 Peter Hendry asked the governors to allow him to take early retirement from the end of August 1984. His decision was based partly on personal reasons and partly because the last of the grammar-school intake had now left. As it turned out, he fell seriously ill with hepatitis and was absent for most of his final term. He had carried out his brief and held the

BELOW LEFT: *Lady Wates with Peter Thomson opening the new junior classrooms, 1987.* RIGHT: *Pupils in the new classrooms built in 1987 – now the modern languages classrooms.*

school together during a period of transition and had done much to restore morale. A gentle and courteous man, he had been a consolidator, leading through consensus. But it was clear that with so much still to be achieved, the school now needed more overt leadership. The governors knew the type of Headmaster they wanted – they expressed a preference for an academic with a good record in sports – and what they wanted him to achieve – to fill the school, lift the standard of sport and improve academic results. From 51 applicants, the shortlist of three included two from the independent sector. Their unanimous choice in December 1983 was Peter Thomson, Surmaster of St Paul's School. Educated at Haileybury, with a first-class honours degree in history from Trinity College, Cambridge, he had taught mainly at St Paul's, with a brief interval at Radley. He had already come across Emanuel for he had been at Radley when, as favourites for the Princess Elizabeth Challenge Cup in 1966, they had been beaten by the school. Tall, handsome and charming, blessed with a memory for names, Thomson proved to be the ideal Headmaster to promote the school to parents and the outside world as well as developing strong links with the Old Emanuels. He was also the man who began carving out an identity for Emanuel as a re-invented independent school. He worked well with the new chairman of governors. Frank Abbott retired early in 1985 and was replaced by Lord Hampden. A descendant of the school's foundress, he had been a governor since 1966.

The new Headmaster, remarked Lord Hampden, 'took the place by storm'. Thomson himself said that 'there was so much to do, it was busy, busy, busy'. With the school roll below 600 when he took over, the first priority had to be to recruit more pupils. Thomson made rapid progress. In just a year numbers had risen to 687 and by the autumn term of 1987 there were 758 boys at the school. A roll of 760 was now accepted as standard. There was a heavy reliance on Assisted Places and as many offers made by the school were rejected as were accepted. But the Hill Form, as the junior form was called, brought in 15 boys every year and the school was also attracting more boys into the fourth, fifth and sixth forms. The financial relief this brought to the school was much appreciated by both governors and the UWF. Emanuel was also helped by the adverse publicity created by strikes in local state schools and by the willingness of some parents to pay fees to secure places where their sons had failed to win Assisted Places.

Part of the reason for this success, particularly in relation to boosting numbers of senior boys, was the way

Peter Thomson, the new Headmaster, unveiling a portrait of Peter Hendry on his retirement (Hendry on right).

Thomson used the system he had inherited, where many boys entered the sixth form to re-sit examinations before either leaving or moving into the upper sixth. 'I was always prepared', recalled Thomson, 'to give any GCE boy a probationary term [in the sixth form].' Initially, this was done out of financial necessity. When some heads of department complained this was weakening academic standards, the Headmaster was frank; he wanted to keep many of these boys not for their academic potential but for their sporting prowess. An admissions policy based largely on a willingness to pay fees and on any sporting or other attributes a boy might have was happily supported by the governors. There were some boys, who had lost their way at other schools, who came to the sixth form in Emanuel and achieved decent results. But the key attraction for many of them was the possibility of taking part in the overseas sporting tours the school organized. Thomson was especially pleased when the sixth form was bolstered by every member of one particularly successful Colts XV.

In fostering sport at Emanuel, Thomson was creating a distinctive reputation for the school based on a tradition epitomized by the victory he had witnessed of the famous rowing eight of 1966, for whom he arranged a special dinner in 1993. Furthermore, while sport brought in the additional boys the school needed for financial stability, sporting success also had the important consequence of boosting morale. The Headmaster led the way, a constant spectator at school matches, with his urgent vocal encouragement of school teams. (He was an equally avid attender of every other school activity as well.) In an era without league tables, and the external scrutiny that came with them, Emanuel could happily bask in the glory achieved by its sportsmen. Much of this can be attributed to the inspiration of Dick Woodall who had joined the school to teach PE and games in 1978 and became head of games in 1985. A fine athlete and an energetic and committed coach, he ran both the first XV and the first XI. It was Woodall

Peter Thomson, Headmaster 1984–94.

Frank Abbott, chairman of the Emanuel School Governing Board, 1963–85.

who first began organizing overseas tours in 1980. A larger than life character, he died young from cancer in 1991 at the age of 38.

Most glorious of all were the school's rowers whose successes had never stopped. Another victory in the Schools Head of the River in 1976 was followed by their first overseas tour, to South Africa. In 1981 the Emanuel first VIII, beaten finalists in the Princess Elizabeth, had been selected to represent Great Britain in the Home Countries' International, recording an easy win under their coach, Richard Marriott. He was succeeded by equally outstanding coaches in Graeme Mulcahy, Mike Partridge, Jeremy Edwards and David Skinner. Both Partridge and Edwards had rowed for Great Britain. In 1985 Sir Ronald Wates and the Wates Foundation generously funded the acquisition of a new boat. Between 1986 and 1988 the first VIII won gold in the National Schools' Regatta, National Championships and European Championships (Coupe de Jeunesse). Among a series of representative honours, two Emanuel boys, Manfred Oberholzer and Robert Morris, rowed for Great Britain in the World Junior Championships and five in the Coupe de Jeunesse. Oberholzer, one of those boys Thomson had persuaded to remain in the sixth form, was selected for the Seoul Olympics in 1988 and rowed with the fourth-placed Great Britain VIII. Another outstanding year was 1991 when the school won gold and silver medals in the finals of the senior quads in the national championships while ten boys won gold medals in the Great Britain championships and represented England in events in Boulogne and Dublin. It was a consistently outstanding record.

Under Woodall, school rugby also enjoyed success, with the school sevens winning the National Westminster Open Tournament in 1979, and in several seasons the first XV won many more matches than it lost. There were rugby tours of Canada in 1981 and California in 1983, followed by a world tour in 1992, covering Singapore, Australia, New

ABOVE: *Emanuel won the London Schools' Knockout Trophy in 1989. Team captain Matthew Coe carries the cup.*

FACING PAGE, MAIN PICTURE: *Sean Maher as Doctor Faustus, 1994.* INSET, BOTTOM, FROM LEFT: *Programme for the production; Production directed by Christian Strover; Scenes for Granada's TV adaptation of* Jeeves and Wooster *were filmed at the school in 1990. Stephen Fry played* Jeeves *and Hugh Laurie,* Bertie Wooster.

BELOW: *Two generations of Emanuel rowers: on left, H W Waddingham, first VIII 1988 and 1989, Gold Medal European Championships, Mantes 1988, Milan 1989; and on right, his father, H Waddingham, first VIII 1958, Chairman of Parents' Association, 1984–7.*

Zealand and Fiji. The Colts XV was unbeaten in 1992–3, winning the county schools championship. The success of the cricket team in 1986 led to an invitation to take part in the Garfield Sobers Trophy in Barbados the following winter. The first XI won the Surrey Cup in 1987 and the Cricketers' Cup three years in a row from 1989. In 1991 the Colts XI won the Barclays Bank competition. The coach of the second XI, Dave Bratt, a former pupil, even revived soccer during the 1980s.

While sport was elevated, culture was overshadowed. Christian Strover, with Simon Gregory, kept the musical flame flickering with choir tours and musicals. Strover's 25th school production, *Annie Get Your Gun*, was staged in 1990, when the school magazine recorded his efforts 'to encourage and develop music and to provide a civilising influence in a world that is only too vulnerable to philistinism and barbarism'.

One of the overseas invitations received by a school team came in 1988 when the junior colts cricketers were invited to Brunei as guests of Prince Abdul-Hakeem. The prince had been a sixth form pupil at the school where he had enjoyed his time so much that he became a generous benefactor. The Head wanted a new sixth form block to celebrate the 400th anniversary of the school in 1994. This would also help the school to continue attracting more boys to the sixth form through the provision of improved facilities which were desperately needed. 'The centre', said the Headmaster, 'was vital to the survival of the sixth form at Emanuel.' It was expected to cost around a million pounds. The governors worried about whether they could afford it. The Head said he hoped to raise part of the cost from an appeal. On that basis, the UWF agreed to fund half. Much of the sum raised through the appeal came from Prince Hakeem. In November 1993 the centre was completed on time and under budget.

This was the major improvement made at the school during this period. There had also been a new classroom block, funded by the UWF in 1985, replacing the embarrassing huts which had been in use for far too long, and other minor improvements, such as the refurbishment of the biology labs and the extension to the boathouse. Otherwise, there was much still to be done. One new master was astonished to find rain pouring through the chapel roof. The anxiety of the governors about funding the sixth form centre showed that the school's finances,

TOP: *Prince Abdul-Hakeem (centre) in the cricket team during his time at Emanuel and* (ABOVE) *Ian Botham playing for the Brunei Old Emanuel XI. In the 1990s an Old Emanuel Select regularly toured Brunei as guests of the prince. The prince brought in 'ringers' such as Ian Botham and Viv Richards who both wore Emanuel colours.* MAIN PICTURE (LEFT): *The school seen from the field. The new sixth form block (on the right) opened in 1994.*

under bursar Alec Jackson and his assistant Jan Kirkup, still had to be managed very carefully. The school was only just breaking even in the early 1990s.

The school's recruitment policy, so successful in raising the number of pupils, had a mixed impact on academic performance. At 'O' level (soon to become GCSE), there were steady improvements during the late 1980s. Ann Thorne, who joined Emanuel in 1987, had one GCSE French set in the early 1990s where every pupil achieved A grades. Staff did work hard to encourage the most able pupils to stay on in the sixth form but 'A' level results were less impressive. The average points score did improve,

Cartoon of Paul Craddock receiving a long-service medal on his retirement, The Portcullis *1982.*

grammar school, an obstacle to further academic improvement. But changing this was made difficult by the almost quasi-independent nature of the common room, dating back to the Grundy years, strengthened during the lack of direction in the Kuper years and never challenged under Hendry, who had himself been part of it. The relationship between Head and common room was not helped by a growing dispute over pay during the late 1980s. This culminated in 1990 with some staff staying away from Speech Day while others deliberately walked in late, to the distress of the Head, the embarrassment of the school's guests and the puzzlement of parents. There had clearly been a breakdown in communications between staff, the Head and governors. The Head never felt the same way about his staff again.

Some notable names disappeared from the school during the 1980s and 1990s. Paul Craddock retired in 1982, followed in 1983 by Arnold Cruise, a supportive second master, and Winifred Turner, who had been appointed as the school's first librarian in 1969. Alan Gilbert, the school

Paul Craddock's tongue-in-cheek school 'report' written by Charles Cuddon to mark his retirement.

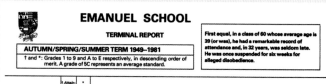

however, and there were years when the school sent several boys to Oxbridge, notably in 1989.

The Head appointed a number of able new teachers to the staff, including several women, although the atmosphere was unsurprisingly but unremittingly masculine. One female teacher who joined Emanuel in 1989 from the state sector thought it was like stepping back in time, where among staff and pupils the status of women was low, the idea of equal opportunities was risible and there was no recognition that women staff existed. 'The only way to survive on the staff at Emanuel', she recalled, 'was to pretend to be a man.' But she found the wide ethnic mix of pupils, many of whom enjoyed strong parental support, was enjoyable if challenging to teach.

Although new appointments were made, the Head failed to tackle the cases of those existing staff who could not or would not adapt to the school's changing circumstances. Parts of the common room were still influenced by the ethos of the past, hanging on to the heritage of the

ABOVE LEFT: *Alan Gilbert, the much-loved school chaplain, died in 1986.* RIGHT: *Charles Cuddon, long-serving and multi-talented English master, retired in 1996. Known as the 'Whitbread man' after featuring on an advertising poster for the beer, Cuddon recalled his favourite remark scrawled on the poster by a pupil when it was hung in the school; 'You can't expect a man to smoke and drink and teach.' His* Dictionary of Literary Terms and Literary Theory *published by Penguin is still in print.*

chaplain for 13 years, whose huge number of godchildren epitomized his essential goodness, died in 1986. Long-serving lab technician Bob Nye retired in 1990 and David Gledhill, who had been on the staff for 25 years, an inspiring teacher of the classics, paternal and kind, erudite and respected, stepped down in 1992. In 1993 Charles Cuddon and Francis Grundy, who as head of maths after Aeron Rogers had continued his scholarship tradition, both retired. Cuddon reflected that the Emanuel common room had rarely been riven by the feuding, cliques or back-biting that often afflicted common rooms elsewhere. Younger members of staff agreed, finding the common room, in the words of one new master, 'extraordinarily welcoming'.

Emanuel had shown its true spirit on 12 December 1988, a bright, beautiful, crisp morning during the last week of term. It was the day of the Clapham rail disaster, when two trains full of early-morning commuters collided on the line below the school. Boys were still arriving at school

while members of the senior management team were in a meeting. The bursar, Alec Jackson, heard 'an enormous explosion, like a bomb, and then smoke – thick, black smog – then absolute mayhem'. In an instant boys were scrambling down the embankment to help, coming across sights they would never wish to see again, while one master took a sledgehammer to the carriage windows to release some of those who were trapped. Then the school swung into action. Boys still arriving were allocated jobs, boys already in school continued to be taught and the Head refused to give up the school to the police, insisting he had a duty of care towards the boys, although he allowed the drive to be taken over. The accident killed 35 people and injured more than 100. Dazed passengers were helped into the school, given tea and coffee, and offered the telephone to make calls to relatives and employers. The ambulances ferrying the injured to hospital were complemented by the school mini-buses. The school dinner ladies provided hot

MAIN PICTURE: *A scene of carnage on a bright winter morning – the Clapham rail disaster, 12 December 1988.* ABOVE: *Mrs Thatcher awarding Terry Stoppani of Emanuel School for his brave actions on the day of the Clapham rail disaster. Terry was one of many boys who helped save the lives of the wounded, every one of them worthy to be known as 'heroes'.*

food at lunchtime for the rescue teams. Emanuel's example moved the nation. The boys were praised by the prime minister, Margaret Thatcher, in the House of Commons, who called them a credit to the country's young people, while the school was visited by the Secretary of State for Education, Kenneth Baker. Peter Thomson spoke of 'my magnificent boys. I am very proud of them'. There was, remembered one member of staff, 'a dreadfully muted atmosphere' in the school for the following week, lifted only when the chaplain conducted an outdoor service on the drive alongside the line. Several boys and members of staff received official recognition for their actions and the school choir was invited to sing alongside the cathedral choir at the memorial service for the victims held in Winchester in January 1989. For several years, the school

whole and for a year they deferred any decision. In 1992, perhaps prompted by a better than expected financial result, the governors re-opened discussions. The committee formed for this purpose was chaired by Francis Abbott, who had joined the governors in 1992 and who was the son of the chairman of governors, Frank Abbott. At the end of the year, staff having reaffirmed their support, the governors agreed that 'if they were going to admit girls then they would have to do it properly'. In May 1993 they decided that girls should be admitted to the sixth form from September 1995 and further consideration should be given to admitting girls throughout the school.

Peter Thomson had intended to leave Emanuel in August 1991 but was persuaded by the governors to stay on until Emanuel's 400th anniversary in 1994. The highlight of that year was a visit by the Queen to the school on 17 March. Thomson had relinquished many of his day-to-day responsibilities in favour of promoting the school and organizing the appeal which coincided with the anniversary. The disadvantage of this decision was that the diversion of the Head from the daily management of the school left Emanuel somewhat adrift like a rudderless ship. But Thomson had made a major contribution towards the renaissance of Emanuel as an independent school. By boosting numbers, he had secured for the governors the

The Emanuel team, gold medal winners at the National Schools' Regatta, 1990 (J16 Quad).

also held an annual lunch for the families of the survivors plus members of the rescue services.

In 1990 the governors debated the possibility of admitting girls to Emanuel for the first time since the 1870s. Support for the idea came from parents, boys at the school who had previously been at co-educational schools, the Old Emanuel Association and staff, who believed girls would have a civilizing effect on Emanuel and boost 'A' level results, particularly in arts subjects. Peter Thomson was even-handed in his approach to the idea and the governors asked him to prepare a feasibility study. One staunch supporter of admitting girls on the governing body was Baroness Dacre, a direct descendant of Anne, Lady Dacre. But there was some uncertainty among the governors as a

U16 Rugby, winners of Hertfordshire and Surrey 7s, 1993.

ABOVE: *Staff photo taken in Peter Thomson's final year as Headmaster, 1994.* BELOW: *Queen Elizabeth II visited the School as part of its 400th anniversary celebrations in 1994.*

income without which the school would not have survived. Although this was partly achieved by reliance on Assisted Places, this was no more than the school had been doing by reliance on LCC scholars in earlier times. At the same time, through his own personality and through fostering a sporting culture attractive to many parents, Emanuel was beginning to rediscover its identity as an independent school. When Thomson left Emanuel at the end of the summer term in 1994, the governors recorded that he had 'almost single-handedly turned the school around and had achieved everything that the governors had asked him to do and more'. Much indeed had been achieved but much more needed to be done.

8

1994 onwards
The Fruits of
Independence

EMANUEL WAS A MORE CONFIDENT school in 1994. The genuine fears that the school might not survive independence had gone. Peter Thomson and his staff had filled Emanuel by creating a distinctive and appealing character for the school. But the emphasis on sport had accentuated Emanuel's uncompromisingly masculine atmosphere which was still reflected in the stark nature of the school buildings. While it was clear that many boys possessed academic potential, there was an obvious weakness in standards, particularly at the top end of the school. The school was financially constrained by its reliance on the Assisted Places Scheme. The governors hoped that the impending admission of girls would both soften the harsher edges of the school and help to improve academic performance. But there were already doubts about the future of Assisted Places and academic results were now exposed to the glare of publicity through the recently introduced school league tables. If Emanuel was to attract fee-paying pupils to replace those on Assisted Places, it was imperative for the school to improve the fabric of the school, widen the scope of the activities it offered and raise academic standards.

Emanuel Choir singing at Ham House National Trust Christmas Concert, 2001.

The governors were clear that their priorities lay in appointing a Head who would tackle unresolved staffing issues and revive academic performance. This was the last appointment in which Frank Abbott took a part. In 1995 he stepped down from the board of governors after a lifetime of service to the school. A former captain of the school, he had joined the board in 1949, becoming chairman in 1963 and serving in that office until 1985, when he had handed over to Lord Hampden. He himself had taken his seat on the retirement of his father, F A Abbott, who had been chairman of the school committee, prior to the formation of a separate board of governors, from 1937 until 1949. With Frank's son already on the board, this was quite a family achievement, stretching over three generations.

Tristram Jones-Parry, Headmaster 1994–8.

Peter Thomson's successor faced quite a challenge. The governors believed Tristram Jones-Parry was just who they were looking for. Educated at Westminster and Christ Church, Oxford, Jones-Parry had taught at Dulwich and Westminster, where his last five years had been spent as Under-Master. He was a tall, quiet, softly spoken man, with a gentle sense of humour, a reluctant public performer whose relaxed, intellectual manner could seem reserved and aloof to those who did not know him. Pupils, however, loved his brilliant performances in the classroom as a maths teacher. A shrewd judge of people, with the interests of the pupils at heart, he was prepared to tackle difficult issues directly and possessed the steely determination to see things through.

He recognized the achievements of his predecessor, particularly the sixth form centre, which would act as a focus for rebuilding the sixth form, but he was dismayed by the physical decrepitude of the place, the buckets in the corridors to catch water, the appalling toilets, the lack of carpets anywhere in the school, and by the low status of music, art and drama. He had a clear grasp of finance and realized at once the need to increase fees for boys who were not on Assisted Places if more rapid physical improvements were to be made. Pastoral care he described to the governors as 'primitive' while the school was lagging behind in the preparation of documentation and the implementation of policies in areas such as health and safety, staff development and appraisal, bullying, personal health and social education and special needs. There was also an acute need for investment in information technology and in the library. He appreciated that many staff were enthusiastic and vigorous in their approach to teaching but it was obvious that some were much less so. Pupil expectations were low so too many boys were failing at both 'A' level and GCSE. He knew the school catered for a wide ability range but believed there was innate potential in every pupil, which was why he was determined that they should all be given the opportunity of moving into the sixth form. Jones-Parry wanted to give academic excellence the same status as sporting excellence but more than that he wanted to make sure that 'every child felt important and had something to contribute'.

BELOW LEFT: *Mary Davies, a loyal and discreet secretary to every Headmaster for over 40 years. She was extremely intrepid, breaking in to the male preserve of the common room and playing a large part in the administration of the school. David Dufour, head of economics, described her as 'a charioteer driving us on' when she retired in 1995.* RIGHT: *Flannels Day, 1994.*

This new approach was critical because the nature of the school's intake began to alter in the early 1990s. The large multi-racial intake which had made the school so distinctive among its peers reflected the coincidence of the Assisted Places Scheme with a change in the character of the local area. Now the area was changing once again. The process of urban decay was being reversed as more affluent professional families, seeking attractive properties at more affordable prices, started to move into Wandsworth and Battersea. This new constituency for the school had different expectations as well as the financial freedom to choose from a wide range of independent day schools. The advent of league tables, the ability of parents to compare the performance of each school, led to increasing competition among south London's day schools. Jones-Parry not only had to look after the interests of the pupils already going through the school, he had to make Emanuel a school which would also appeal to the new families moving into the area. In other words, Emanuel, as a local school, had to respond to the needs of the local area which it served.

This tied in with the need to plan for the likely abolition of the Assisted Places Scheme. The school needed more pupils coming into the school at 11 or over but also a larger sixth form. This depended on a higher standard of entry and the improvement of academic results through able staff stretching pupils to their full potential. Jones-Parry signalled his intentions from the very start by announcing several staff redundancies and appointing able teachers in their place. At the same time the governors agreed to raise

Girls were admitted to the sixth form in 1995. Shown here are the first cohort of girls to have gone all the way through the school from year 7 to the upper sixth.

the bar for entry into the school. If Assisted Places were to disappear, however, the school also needed to make better provision through more bursaries to continue Emanuel's tradition of educating able children from poor backgrounds.

This complex transformation meant it would prove particularly difficult at first for the school to recruit boys into the junior forms and at 11 until academic performance did improve; on the other hand, Jones-Parry was successful in raising the proportion of pupils staying on in the sixth form from around a quarter in 1994 to about two-thirds by 1998. Interest in the school was stimulated through the very successful Open Days organized by Jeremy Edwards, the issue of a new prospectus and visits to local primary schools. The school made the most of those physical advantages it had – the secure site, the local playing fields and the swimming pool.

The admission of girls was intended to be an important part of sustaining numbers. The governors decided that girls would be admitted throughout the school from September 1996. By the autumn of 1997, there were 23 girls in the sixth form and another 40 spread between the junior forms and the first two years in the senior school. But like so many other boys' schools that first opened their doors to girls, Emanuel was still just a boys' school with girls. The governors seriously underestimated the physical and cultural changes which needed to be made before the school

Girls were readmitted to the lower school in 1996.

Pupils enjoy taking part in many trips organised by the school.

could be called truly co-educational. Few concessions were made to those first girls, Mita Desai, Sarah Denny, Yasman Ghomshei and Janine Nolan, who joined the sixth form in September 1995. Janine Nolan later wrote how 'for the first week we endured ignorance, bewilderment and curiosity and, sad to say, the girls' locker room became our favourite refuge'. The girls decided that attack was the best form of defence and took on the boys on their own turf, playing badminton and taking up rowing, although for several months they had to put up with 'immature idiocies' from a handful of lower sixth form boys. 'We shared a determination not to be beaten and, with much support, we stayed.' They were helped by the admission of girls throughout the school from the following year and it was this intake in particular which would ultimately prove to have a more civilizing influence on the sixth form. In the meantime, however, the girls had to be almost as tough as the boys to hold their own, making them daunting opposition for visiting teams. But the way they had no truck with aggressive male attitudes slowly began to change the atmosphere of the place.

Pastoral care had a part to play in this process too. It was excellent in the lower school under Jeremy Edwards and remained so under his successor, Sue Neale. Edwards was then transferred to improve the standard of care in the middle school. Involving himself with the boys, he helped them form work habits,

TOP: *Pupils abseiling.* BOTTOM: *Cycling on activity camps.*

made them feel confident in their ability to achieve and restored their sense of self-worth. Jones-Parry also introduced heads of year for the first time. Special needs specialists were employed to identify and assist pupils with particular problems. Sex and drugs education was introduced. Ann Thorne was responsible for bringing in a series of challenging speakers to talk to the sixth form.

Improving the physical environment and extending the facilities offered by the school was also important, not only if the school wished to attract more girls, but also if Emanuel wanted to appeal to the changing population of its local catchment area. In partnership with the new bursar, Jan Kirkup, Jones-Parry also made a start on improving facilities and bringing the school fabric up to date. Work started on refurbishing classrooms and modernizing science laboratories. The school toilets were transformed. Flowers appeared and carpets were laid down. A buttery was created by covering over an internal courtyard as a space where pupils could eat sandwiches. A new librarian, Marianne Bradnock, was appointed to overhaul the library. Although the staff always believed the Head had little time for sport, it was Jones-Parry who began thinking about the possibility of a purpose-built sports hall. In fact, Emanuel sustained its sporting reputation, developing increasing breadth, with the addition of more sports as girls joined the school, producing several outstanding team and individual achievements.

Jones-Parry was also determined to do something about the poor provision for music. The creation of the buttery freed the junior dining hall for conversion into music facilities. In May 1997 two schemes were placed before the governors, who, showing a lack of confidence in sharp contrast to the ambitions of the Head, opted for the lesser of the two, expressing concern over the future of numbers as the new government announced the end of Assisted Places. As Christian Strover said farewell after 42 years, Jonathan Holmes was appointed as director of music. While the school's choral tradition owed much to Strover, encouragement was now given to chamber and orchestral music. New directors of drama and art were also appointed.

In 1998 Jones-Parry was asked to return to Westminster as Headmaster. The governors regretted his departure. An HMC inspection of the school at the beginning of the year measured his contribution to Emanuel. He had striven to

Lily Bolton-Green, a talented Emanuel athlete who played for Queen's Park Rangers.

raise expectations and standards, improve the buildings, pastoral care and managerial effectiveness. Most pupils, wrote the inspectors, were capable of good levels of achievement, taught by a balanced staff, with many new appointments. The pupils were open, direct and down to earth, and there was 'a clear sense of a living community and a high degree of mutual respect, liking and co-operation'. Further work was required on academic standards and staffing, improving the environment, integrating girls and marketing the school, but the changes made by the Head, concluded the inspectors, had had 'a dramatic effect on the sense of purpose, on morale and on levels of achievement'. Jones-Parry had laid down yet another building block in the reconstruction of Emanuel's independent identity.

In his place the governors appointed Emanuel's first woman Head, Anne-Marie Sutcliffe. The chairman of governors was clear that she was appointed on merit and not because the governors wanted a woman Head to integrate girls fully into the school. Although she did not have the personal presence of her predecessor, she was sharp,

Girls first VIII competing in the Schools Head of River race, 2005.

personable and approachable, with a relish for teaching and a clear sense of purpose. She had taught in both the state and independent sectors, eventually becoming head of history at St Paul's Girls' School and then deputy head at Channing School. She quickly realized the challenge which faced her. Firstly, a fellow candidate for the post withdrew in the belief that, having studied the figures, the risk of Emanuel failing was too great. Secondly, despite the best efforts of Jones-Parry, she found the school buildings were still 'scruffy and smelly'. She was also amazed to discover that not one head of department was a woman. The trouble Emanuel had had in finding its feet since independence was obvious to her. She believed that even in 1998 Emanuel was still 'very uneasily poised … it did not really know what it was'.

Sorting out the school's academic performance was bound to increase Emanuel's self-confidence and for Anne-Marie Sutcliffe it was a priority to continue the work begun by her predecessor. She decided that standards must now have precedence over numbers. This was a brave decision to take at a time when the Assisted Places Scheme was winding down and competition among south London day schools was increasing. The Headmistress was particularly keen to make further improvements in sixth form standards. She appointed a new head of sixth form, Richard Marriott, who had returned to the school, and he proceeded to transform the approach of pupils towards work and behaviour. The Head had also insisted in her first year that the minimum requirement for sixth form entry was five GCSEs, including English and maths. One of the consequences of this was indeed a decline in overall numbers, particularly in the sixth form, and it was a constant struggle to find more fee-paying pupils. Emanuel continued to face the problem that while it remained essential to maintain numbers, it was difficult to be very selective about annual admissions since the school still did not have the standing locally to attract the most able pupils. The result of all this was that although Emanuel succeeded in replacing more than 200 Assisted Places with fee-paying pupils, there were almost 80 fewer pupils in 2004 than here had been in 1998. But clearly the Headmistress was right in the decisions she made. Her hope was that standards would continue to improve, increasing the attraction of the school for more able potential pupils.

THIS AND FACING PAGE, CLOCKWISE FROM TOP LEFT: *Anne-Marie Sutcliffe, Headmistress 1998–2004; Jonathan Westmore and Missie Frank in* Othello, *2004; Rehearsing for* The Lion King; *Meera Shaunak playing cello; Emanuel choir performing at Segur de Calafell in Spain; Emanuel pupils participated in Verdi's* Requiem.

Part of this process also involved the further development of the standard of teaching at Emanuel. The Head appreciated that most of the teaching in the school was generally good. Some aspects were outstanding. Her predecessor, for instance, had been so impressed with the way in which design technology was taught under Cliff Lynn that he adopted it as a template for Westminster. But the Head was also aware that there was room for further improvement. So, supported by Jeremy Edwards who became deputy head in 1995, she accelerated the process begun by her predecessor in sorting the wheat from the chaff. Those staff whose poor performance contributed towards poor behaviour both inside and outside the classroom left the school. There was a constant stream of new appointments, so staff became younger, more open, more flexible and more receptive to change. More women were appointed, often to senior posts (today women are heads of English, modern languages, chemistry, biology and physics), reinforcing the reality that Emanuel was once again a co-educational school. In 2000 two staff were deliberately appointed from the state sector, on the grounds that their work ethic and ability to handle change would be an example to others. Bill Rogers came from Wallington

Marcus Altman in the art studio, 2006.

County Grammar School as director of studies and John Hardy from Langley Parks Boys' School to replace Edwards as deputy head. They were both amazed to find a school that was, in Hardy's words, 'like the land that time forgot', despite all the changes it had undergone during the previous two decades. The pace of modernization was quickened. In-service training was properly established for the first time and contributed towards instituting a more appropriate system of discipline throughout the school, including uniform, time-keeping, courtesy and the correct requirements for lessons. Conduct cards became more a vehicle for commendations and praise than criticism. As a result the standard of behaviour throughout the school improved significantly. A school council was also formed which saw Emanuel jettison junk food long before Jamie Oliver's campaign. Pastoral care was improved with closer monitoring of the progress of every pupil. Target setting, progress reports based on effort and achievement and a broad programme of learning support were introduced to boost academic performance. Staff began working towards agreed common goals, a team ethos was encouraged and communications throughout the school were improved. The benefits began to percolate through the school so that by 2001 91 per cent of all pupils were achieving A*–C grades at GCSE, although this advance had yet to reach 'A' levels.

The Head was also helped in her aims for Emanuel by the move in 1999 towards 'a higher-fees, higher-spend' strategy. Although there had been some change under Jones-Parry, Emanuel's fees were still low in comparison with similar schools. The theory was that this made the school more attractive, thus maintaining numbers, but this was clearly not the case. In fact, low fees starved the school of the income required to make those improvements which would truly make Emanuel more attractive to parents. The time had come, as Assisted Places disappeared, to raise fees in line with those of nearby competitors. This decision was immediately followed by the agreement of the governors to press ahead with the construction of the sports hall. The music department, begun under Jones-Parry, was completed. Further refurbishment of the laboratories, a better boathouse, the rebuilding of the common room, the installation of a modern telephone system and cabling network and an improved reception area quickly followed. New chemistry laboratories were opened by one of the school's most famous former pupils, Peter Goddard, in

CLOCKWISE FROM TOP LEFT: *Will Greenwood, Anne-Marie Sutcliffe, Ben Kelly (school rugby captain) and Lord Hampden at the opening of the sports hall, 2003; the new refectory; the fitness suite in the new sports hall.* BELOW: *Baroness Dacre at the service of thanksgiving to mark the 400th anniversary of granting the Emanuel Hospital Charter in Chelsea Old Church, 2001.*

October 1999. Will Greenwood, the international rugby player, opened the sports hall in February 2003. The former gym was transformed into a modern cafeteria, with new kitchens, plus meeting rooms and an improved pavilion.

When the Head was asked what she would like to see next in the school, she replied 'a really good library in the heart of the school'. She did much to foster the cultural ethos of the school, building on the work of her predecessor. Under Marianne Bradnock and her successor as librarian, Tony Jones, the school had begun to attract a string of renowned authors who came to talk to the pupils about their books. Arts Week was also a great success and the standard of music, drama and art, under dedicated directors, flourished. She instituted scholarships for art and music and by the time she left there were 33 art and 22 music scholars. As the school magazine later noted, all this showed 'what a thriving, healthy and exciting place Emanuel has become'.

It was obvious to the Headmistress, with her sense of history, that Emanuel's character and ethos were underpinned by its origins. She made this plain in 2001 on the occasion of the 400th anniversary of the granting of the Emanuel Hospital charter. This was marked by several events, including a service of thanksgiving in Chelsea Old Church. The Headmistress emphasized how the school existed to provide an excellent and diverse education,

The new library opened in May 2007. The opening was attended by, among others (TOP, FROM LEFT): Francis Abbott, the current chairman of governors and Lord Hampden, chair of governors from 1985 to 2004; Mike Markland, Michael Mills and Derek Saunders. MAIN PICTURE: Pupils in the library, 2008.

encouraging respect for every pupil, enabling each one to develop his or her potential. This ethos was clearly linked to the provisions of Lady Dacre's will, encompassing virtue – through the development of a personal moral code, self-respect, responsibility and independence, care and consideration for others; the good and laudable arts – the achievement of academic and cultural excellence, the acquisition of confidence, fluency and knowledge, of physical, social and practical skills; and living by honest labour – enabling pupils to enter higher education, pursue careers, and serve as citizens. She turned the past into an asset for the future; the school no longer had the need to look back, it now had the confidence to look forward. As a member of staff wrote when Anne-Marie Sutcliffe stepped down in 2004, 'it is not enough to rely on the glory of a distant and tenuous vision of a mythical past. The school is now forward thinking as opposed to backward looking and that is why it is such an exciting place to be. Much of this is down to her'.

The truth was that after six years of hard work and total commitment to the school, the Headmistress had worn herself out. She told the governors to their regret in 2003 that she would leave at the end of the summer term in 2004. Testament to the change she made came from the chairman of governors, Lord Hampden. She enjoyed a warm and close working relationship with him although she felt that the governing body as a whole still remained too disengaged from the school. Lord Hampden said that he would walk down the school drive, an unknown figure to the pupils, watching their faces. Most of the time they were happy and smiling, reflecting their enjoyment of school life. Anne-Marie Sutcliffe had, in his words, 'made the school a really happy place … and a very friendly place'.

She was aware, as had been each of her predecessors since independence, that while much had been done, there was was still much to do. But Emanuel's self-confidence was now stronger than it had ever been. There was a feeling of momentum within the school which had been steadily growing under each successive Head, enabling the school to keep on surging forward despite the fact that there had been three changes at the top in a decade.

The new Headmaster who took over in September 2004 was Mark Hanley-Browne, energetic and enthusiastic, the outstanding candidate, who came from Highgate School where he had been deputy head. He appreciated the

Working in the new library.

progress made by the school, believing that Emanuel was 'already a school on the way up'. The buildings had been transformed over the past few years and the new Head was keen to press ahead with the idea already mooted for a new library at the heart of the school as his first project. This elegant modern facility was opened in May 2007. He also continued a policy of making the interior of the school warmer and more welcoming, filling the walls with works of art by pupils and with photographs illustrating the diverse range of activities they pursued at school. He employed additional staff to improve the grounds and took down all the notices forbidding pupils to walk on the grass – if the school had attractive grounds, then the pupils should be able to enjoy them. He also built on the outstanding quality of music, drama and art at Emanuel.

ABOVE: *Members of the highly successful boys U13 rugby team coached by Glen Cassidy. The U13 sevens team were runners up in the National Sevens championships at Rosslyn Park in 2008.* BELOW (RIGHT): *Year 10 Boys' Rowing VIII, 2008.*

Drama is now taught from year 6 onwards and a new theatre has been created in the space vacated by the old library. Drama scholarships, still rare in London schools, were added to the music and art scholarships.

Despite the addition of the new sports hall, sport had been relatively neglected as the focus of attention had been switched to other areas of the school. This has been addressed partly by the appointment of additional sports coaches. The school now uses Blagdons almost every Saturday throughout the winter, sharing the facilities with Westminster City School. The ground is used on weekday mornings by Harlequins rugby club. Soccer has been relegated to restore excellence in rugby which, with rowing, has adopted professional training regimes. In relation to Westminster City School, the Headmaster has been enthusiastic in forging stronger links between the

school and Emanuel through UWS. This relationship has attracted considerable interest, including from government, during the debate over the past few years about the need for independent schools enjoying charitable status to demonstrate public benefit.

A message which the Head has tried to get across to pupils is that constant commitment brings success and it is this which the Head wishes to embed in the classroom. He knew that the school already possessed a staff of undoubted calibre, commitment and professionalism, such as Harry Jackson, who had done much to improve the quality of careers advice, John Layng, who became director of rowing and assistant director of studies, Jonathan Driver, later chairman of the common room, who had been at the school since 1989, and Chris Labinjo who would work alongside Richard Marriott and Jo Pattman in the sixth form. The challenge was to further strengthen the Common Room and to raise the self-confidence of the pupils, so they could face their personal challenges with the belief that they could be overcome. Above all, however, the Head wanted to stress that Emanuel was about excellence in many spheres, that it was a school focused on the happiness of each individual child, that it could help to develop the potential of every pupil, whether in the classroom, on the sports field, stage or concert platform or any area of activity. This message was emphasized, for instance, through the institution of an annual dinner for the holder of every scholarship in the school. Sophia MacMillan, director of art since 2000, was appointed director of the scholars to oversee all the activities involving the scholars which now take place throughout the year.

TOP: *The South Courtyard opened in 2008. The tree was planted by Queen Elizabeth in 1951 and visited by her daughter, the present Queen Elizabeth, in 1994.* BOTTOM, (FROM LEFT): *Working in the archive section of the library; In between lessons; Rehearsing in the theatre.*

Under Mark Hanley-Browne, the chapel has also been restored and, under the new chaplain, Paul Hunt, the spiritual aspect of the school has been reclaimed from the sidelines and is beginning to form an integral part of Emanuel's constantly evolving scheme of pastoral care.

More effort has also been invested in the true integration of girls within the school. A senior tutor for girls, Sara Williams-Ryan, was appointed in 2004 and improvements since then have covered everything from working locks in the changing rooms and hairdryers at the swimming pool to a girls' focus group which meets twice a term and new clubs, covering fashion, yoga and dance, which more properly reflected their interests. This has all helped to boost their self-confidence and make them equal members in the school.

THIS AND FACING PAGE: *The distinctive boards outside the chapel with the Lord's Prayer and the Creed.*

There were also changes in the governing body. Lord Hampden retired in 2004, along with Baroness Dacre, with respective service of 39 and 32 years to the school. The important links with the Dacre family were maintained by the appointment of Baroness Dacre's nephew, Jamie Douglas-Home, to the board. Francis Abbott took over as chairman and is keenly aware of the need for the governors to be more intimately involved with the school. This process has been aided by the interest taken by the chairmen of key committees, including Marion Parsons, who chairs the curriculum committee, Bryan Baughan, chair of the finance committee, and Catherine McGuinness, chair of the personnel committee. The expertise in the construction industry of two other governors, Paul Kennerley and James Wates, the latter continuing a long family association

Mark Hanley-Browne with senior prefects in his study, 2007.

with Emanuel, has also been very valuable. Two other new members, Dr Patrick Zutshi of Cambridge University and Dr David Ricks of King's College, London, bring academic expertise to the governors.

Better facilities, excellence in art, music and drama, the continued improvement in academic and sporting results, plus the self-confidence this engendered within the school, has made Emanuel more and more attractive. As the surrounding neighbourhood has continued to improve materially, the school has drawn an increasing number of applicants for places every year with the obvious future benefit for the school's academic performance. The school has also improved its interviewing and testing procedures, in which Simon Gregory, Paul McMahon and John Benn have played a major part. The roll, with around 700 pupils, has more than recovered from the dip it previously experienced. The further work on integrating girls within the school has ensured that Emanuel has also become the co-educational independent school of choice locally. There is now a very active parental involvement in the school through the Parents' Association which is closely involved with the annual organization of Dacre Day. Debbie Barty-King and Jenny Jefferis have played a major role in recent years, latterly handing over to Colin Russell and Rosie Shepperd. For them and for many families the overriding attraction of the school remains the broad range of opportunities which Emanuel confidently offers to their

The Creed. This board, taken from the Old Emanuel Chapel in Westminster, is now displayed on the staircase leading up to the Chapel at Emanuel School.

children. As a member of the Parents' Association put it, Emanuel 'recognizes that children flower in different ways'.

The links between Emanuel and the origins of the school more than 400 years ago have already been outlined above. These are an intrinsic part of the school today which is probably more confident in itself and more sure of its own identity than it has ever been. The school has on several occasions struggled to find its identity. Its most successful periods have been those where it has benefited from a clear and consistent lead, given in the first instance under Cyril Broom from 1928 until 1953 and then, under several different Heads but over a similar period of time, from independence onwards after 1976. The problems of a shifting catchment area, lack of money, conflict with government and local authorities, which for so long plagued the fortunes of the school are now increasingly dim memories. Today the school, clear about its role within the local community, no longer has the need to hark back to the past for fear of what the future might hold. Emanuel School can proudly embrace the past – the sporting tradition, the broad range of activities catering for every child, the concept of the school as a corporate family, the central role of the chapel in school life, the continuing links with the descendants of the founders – for the part which it plays in today's school. It is now a winning combination.

School Roll 2008

GOVERNORS

Francis Abbott – *Chairman*
Bryan Baughan
Susan Chambers
Jamie Douglas-Home
Howard Hughes
Paul Kennerley
Catherine McGuinness – *Vice Chairman*
Melissa D'Mello
Marion Parsons
David Ricks
Stephen Roberts
Claude Scott
Trevor Smith
James Wates
Patrick Zutshi

Roy Blackwell – *Clerk to the Foundation*

SENIOR ACADEMIC STAFF

Mark Hanley-Browne – *Headmaster*
John Hardy – *Second Master*
Bill Rogers – *Director of Studies*
Richard Marriott – *Head of Sixth Form*
John Benn – *Head of the Middle School and Senior Tutor*
Simon Gregory – *Head of the Junior School*
Sara Williams-Ryan – *Head of MFL and Senior Tutor for Girls*
Paul Hunt – *Chaplain*
Derek Taylor – *Director of Finance*

ACADEMIC STAFF

Shaun Andrews – *HoY, History*
Andrew Ball – *HoD, Design Technology*
Richard Berlie – *HoD, History*
Janet Bettesworth – *Art*
Sean Bettinson – *Director of Sport*
Edward Braun – *Design Technology*
Lisa Brown – *English*
Henny Burnett – *Art*
Lucy Butler – *Psychology*
Glen Cassidy – *HoH, Maths*

Lisa Cleveland – *HoD, Religious Studies*
Rosie Collins – *Learning Support*
Malcolm Dancy – *Physics*
Gary Dibden – *HoH, Assistant Librarian*
Jonathan Driver – *HoH, Societies, History*
Stuart Fairlamb – *Design Technology*
Nayeem Fazaluddin – *HoD, Maths*
Laura Fitzgibbon – *Assistant Director of Sport, HoH*
Geraldine Fornari – *HoD, Learning Support*
Alan Friell – *PE and games*
Steve Halliwell – *English, Editor of* The Portcullis
Jennifer Halsey – *Maths*
Dougal Hand – *English*
Michael Healy – *Biology*
Jo Henderson – *English*
Jonathan Holmes – *HoD, Music*
Sarah Holmes – *Music*
Bernard Howard – *Director of ICT*
Harry Jackson – *HoD, German*
Monica Jimenez – *Spanish and French*
Tony Jones – *Senior Librarian*
Andrew Keddie – *History and Politics*
Amber Kennedy – *PE and games*
Raj Khuman – *Physics*
Paul King – *HoH, Master i/c cricket, Physics*
Chris Labinjo – *HoY, Biology*
Brian Last – *HoD, Drama*
Joanne Lawton – *Maths*
John Layng – *Assistant Director of Studies, HoH, Biology*
Vincent le Gac – *HoH, French*
Rachel Lewis – *French*
Frances Lindsey-Clark – *French*
Ofelia Lopez – *HoY, Exams, Geography*
Sophia MacMillan – *HoD, Art, Director of the Scholars*
Catriona Maher – *HoD, Chemistry*
Huma Malik – *Careers, Chemistry*
Geraldine Marmion – *Maths*
Philomena Marmion – *Maths and Design Technology*

Richard Marriott – *Head of Sixth, Maths*
Paul McMahon – *HoY, Geography*
Jane Morrison-Bartlett – *Head of Science, Physics*
Neil Mullen – *HoD, Classics*
Rachel Musson – *English*
Asaad Noori – *HoD, ICT*
Jo Pattman – *HoD, English*
Bill Purkis – *HoD, Geography*
Kostas Ragkousis – *ICT*
Barbara Reynolds – *HoD, Biology*
Bill Rogers – *Director of Studies, Chemistry*
Olga Roncero-Refoyo – *Exams, Spanish*
Rick Skinner – *Maths and rowing*
Mark Sowden – *HoY, PE and games*
Matthew Swift – *Art*
Carl Thomas – *Chemistry*
Rupert Tong – *HoD, Economics and Business Studies*
Gina Wright – *HoD, Psychology*
Michelle Yan – *HoY, Classics*
Anabel Zaratiegui – *HoD, Spanish*

SPORTS COACHES

Fred Badowski – *Rowing*
Sam Gourevitch – *Rowing*
Alison Elliott – *Rowing*
Max Garth – *Rugby*
Dominique Redmond – *Fives*
Howard Wiseman – *Fives*

SPECIALIST MUSIC TEACHERS

Fabian Beard
Finlay Crowther
Michael Crowther
Patricia Crowther
Jacqueline Hayter
Alan Kendall
Katrina Lauder
Eliza Marshall
Anna Piatgorsky
Rachel Philips
Roy Schunter
Lynn Selwood
Pavan Sharda

Naomi Shephard
Helen Twomey
John Webb

ADMINISTRATIVE SUPPORT STAFF

Mark Benbow – *Head Groundsman*
Jenny Bonner – *Catering Manager*
Nora Browne – *Common Room Secretary*
Paul Counsell – *School Keeper*
Gary Dibden – *Assistant Librarian*
Richard England – *Chef*
Sarah Fisher – *Marketing Director*
Linda Gomez – *School Secretary*
Graham Halliday – *Maintenance*
Elizabeth Hogan – *Finance Assistant*
Bernard Howard – *Director of ICT*
Denise Jackman – *Chemistry Technician*
Peter Joseph – *Network Manager*
Gerald King – *Physics Technician*
Jan Kirkup – *Project Manager*
John Legg – *Sports Hall Attendant*
Billy McAuliffe – *Finance Officer and Accountant*
Jean Nicholls – *Chemistry Technician*
Tony Norton – *Assistant School keeper*
Mediana Philp – *Reception*
Gary Pooley – *Estates Manager*
Lindsay Sabin – *School nurse*
Debra Shuttleworth – *Admissions Secretary*
Julian Wolchover – *Design Technology technician*
Alan Wood – *Maintenance*
Jill Wood – *Headmaster's Secretary*
Graham Woodland – *Biology Technician*

SCHOOL PREFECTS

Luke Dyson – *Head Boy*
Micaela Wing – *Head Girl*
Dominic Murphy – *Deputy Head Boy*
Cecilia Redondo Zaratiegui – *Deputy Head Girl*
Polly Aitman
Celia Burton
Chris Chilton
Josh Coller
Chris Edwards
Robbie Hamilton
Ramsey Ipe
Hannah Majewska
Lawrence Matini
Symone McEachron
Ben Newton
Tom Rowson
Henry Shiplee
John Symeon
Rebecca Thomas
Jenna Walters

UPPER SIXTH

Polly Aitman
Ibrahim Ali
Farran Anstock
Aatif Ashraf
Thomas Bacon
Mayling Barr
Tomi Biberovic
Celia Burton
Angus Carter
Otto Castle
Luca Cavalli
Christopher Chilton
George Clarke-Hackston
Edward Cole
Joshua Coller
Graham Cooper
Margeaux Creaturo
Charlie d'Auria
Marcus Desai
Sarah Duffy
Luke Dyson
Christopher Edwards
Sam Frankl-Bertram
Suzanne Geddes
Robbie Hamilton
Jimmy Harriott
Ruth Hastie-Oldland
Robert Hervais-Adelman
Florence Hunter
Finlay Hutchison
Ramsey Ipe
Akhil Kapur
Theo Keane
Rory Lampier

Stefan Lazic
Frederika Little
Emer McCoy
Symone McEachron
Imogen McRoberts
Hannah Majewska
Samuel Martin-Thomas
Lawrence Matini
Alun Meredith
Dominic Murphy
Ben Newton
Haseeb Quraishi
Cecilia Redondo Zaratiegui
Tom Rowson
Cole Salewicz
Christy Salter
James Salvesen
David Schofield
Isobel Scott
William Sharkey
Henry Shiplee
William Slater
Rory Summerley
John Symeon
Michael Teale
Rebecca Thomas
Michael Tong
Scott Townsin
Christianne van Besouw
Richard Vuong
Jenna Walters
Stuart Wavell
Harry Whiteley
Micaela Wing

LOWER SIXTH

Sajeel Ahmed
Richard Allen
Jaimin Amin
Gevork Areshyan
Zakia Bajwa
Louis Beazley
Martin Bennie
Rosalind Bown
Sam Bradford-Smith
Christopher Braithwaite
Jack Brown
Jamal Brown-Watts
India Brummitt
Jordan Burton
Lily Cheley
Paul Chilton
Nicholas Collett
Alex Cross
Katy Dillon
Harry Docherty White
Tashan Dunbar
Arthur Duncan
Jamie Farrimond
Oscar Featherstone

William Finney
Isobel Fitzgerald
Max Fowler
Joshua Freeman
Alexander Goldsworthy
Adam Goodwin
Joseph Hand
Laurence Handy
Christopher Hills
Sam Hood
Laura Horseman
Jack Hutchings
Anthony Ing
Lauren Jefferis
Maria Johnston
Maja Jovicevic
Natasha Kearns
Nathan Kent
Ismael Khan
Toby Lampier
Amy Launder
Matthew Leeks
Robbie McKane
James McLoughlin
Sam Mardon
James Mathew
Stephen Mayhew
William Moult
Sarah Mullen
Madeeha Mustafa
Charlie Newey
Dominic Newman
Tasha O'Byrne
Jermaine Olasan
Tom Osborne
Samuel Parkinson
Ayesha Patel
Nimesh Patel
Kristiana Patsalos
Rose Priddy
Matthew Pyne
Mair Roberts
Samson Saunders
Jess Sestili
Charlie Shackleton-Lyne
Abdul Sheikh
Katy Sherratt
Adam Skinner
Frederick Smart
Polly Snowdon
Kieron Stewart
Zoe Thomas-Webb
William Tilzey
James Tipler
George Tripp
Edward Ursell
Joe Venning
Patrick Walford
Toby Watson
Jack Willett
George Wilson

Alex Yacoub

YEAR 11

Molly Ackhurst
Daniel Aldred
Lucy Andrews
Arman Arya
Nabil Aslam
Izzy Aspeling-Jones
Charlie Barrett
Callum Black
Alexander Boag
Jordan Braddock
Lucy Brandon
Shakira Browne
Thomas Burch
Nell Campbell
Joe Chadwick
Kane Chandler-Symons
Hiren Chauhan
Mags Chilaev
Ji-Hye Choi
Matthew Conn
David Connor
Alim Datoo
Ben Davy
Elyssa Desai
Sean Donaghy
Emma Dudlyke
Laura Dyson
Daniel Emam
Oliver Evans
Christopher Fahmy
Phoebe Fisher
Ruby Gaskell
Emily Gilmour
Charlie Griffiths
Simon Harris
Clare Harrison
Sam Hawley
David Howell
Sophie Jenkins
Julian Jest
Thomas Joannou
Jovana Jovicevic
Luke Keane
Declan Kolakowski
Jamil Lalani
Guido Lanteri Laura
Jonty Lees
Dominic Leigh
Ashraf Ludhi
Catriona Maclean
Alastair McRae
Camilla Mason
Millar Maxwell
Daniel Meekings
Georgia Miansarow
Nishant Modasia
Daniel Moodliar

Ellie Moore
Bethan Morris
Percy Neville-Johnson
Adam Newton
Gerard O'Reilly
Seung-kyu Park
Tabitha Perry
James Phokela-Lees
Jake Plastow-Chason
Hugo Realfonzo
Angus Reynolds
Ted Riley
Su Ripley
Lily Robertson
Charles Rutter
Jim Samengo-Turner
Oyinka Sanusi
Ben Schumann-Nixon
William Sharp
India Shaw
Isabella Shaw
Matthew Smith
George Steer
Alex Taylor
Aaron Tsui
Lana Vukojicic
Andrew Vuong
Charlie Whiteley
Oliver Willis
Gabrielle Winwood
George Wolstenholme

Year 10

Eraaz Ali
Yasmin Ayoub
Alfie Baker
Zakary Barakat
Charlie Barty-King
Oliver Bell
Louis Bennett
Ellie Blackburn
Ella Blewitt
Ella Brimelow
Benjamin Brown
Hannah Burles
Tumaini Carayol
Rupert Cheetham
Stella Collinson
Alexander Creaturo
Mia Cupic
Spike Dammers
Feyisope Debo-Aina
Mahsa Dehghani
Vivienne Delliou-Daly
Stefan Denic
Natasha Djukic
Josh Donaldson-Colls
Matthew Dunford
Gus Forrest
James Forward

Serador Gabriel
Fanuel Getachew
Katherine Gordon
Felix Greenhalgh
Rory Grieve
Felix Gudin-Williams
Jonno Hall
Oliver Halls
Maddie Harriott
Helen Hobson
Jack Hodsoll
Luke Jackson-Mackay
Isaac Kimbugwe
Freddie Kingsmill
Joseph Lampier
Tayo Lawal
Elliot Liston
Patrick Lufkin
Calum McCulloch
Rosie Mackay
Georgina Maclachlan
Amy Maclean
Alexander Madigan
Alexander Malinowski
Charlotte Marsh
Oliver Matini
Kai Matthews
Hitesh Mavjee
Abigail Mayhew
Guy Medawar
Kathryn Meredith
Jamie Miller
James Morrison-Bartlett
Tess Moujaes
Timmy Newman
Daniel Nicholson
Oliver Page
Saul Parkinson
Vinit Patel
Joe Philip
Ben Rawlins
Kiman Read
Sean Rigley
Ben Rimerici
Alastair Ross
Claudia Russell
Rex Russell
Lara Sampson
Adam Sandford
Komali Scott Jones
Lucy Shiplee
Nichola Simpson
Ella Sparks
Sam Stanier
Oliver Stokes
Hamesh Thaker
Luke Thompson
Carla Tipler
Patrick Townsin
Poppy Turner
Kit Venning

Tatchiana Whalley
Caspian Whistler
Stephanie White
Meghan Willcox
Jonathan Wilson
Sophie Wilson
Jamie Yuksel

Year 9

Rosalind Adams
Joshua Aitman
Robert Akehurst
Hugo Allen
Albbie Amankona
Dominic Anderson
Constance Attlee
Fergus Attlee
Callum Bain
Helen Bennie
Jacob Bierer-Nielsen
Ryan Bourgi
Jaik Bramley-Fenton
Archie Campbell
Claudia Castle
Bertie Chapman
Hyuk-Soon Choi
Henry Cole
Edward Coles
Oliver Conte
Michael Costa
Callum Counihan
Claudia Cretella
Alvin Daramola-Rose
Luca Davenport
Ollie Davey
Daniel David
Robert Davies
Natalie Dean
Jack Delaney
Chris Desira
Zoe Dickey
Olivia Ditcham
Daniel Ebrahim
George Elliott
Nicholas Emmett
Joshua Eppel
Daniel Ferree
Caroline Finney
Jack Fontaine
Fred Fox
Claudette Gaia
Walter Gaskell
Zac Gasson
Nicholas Gillingwater
Oscar Granstrom-Livesey
Clare Grenville
Jake Grewal
Erkan Gursel
Michael Hallifax
Usayeed Haque

Eliza Hatch
James Hawkins
Harry Hickman
Alice Hill
Saabir Hossain
Isabel Hunter
Frederick Ikezue-Clifford
Julia Jefferis
Tom Jelliffe
Sepehr Karimpour
Oliver Lalani
Sam Lee
James Leech
Edward Letch
Anna Lewis-Purkis
Nicholas Lowe
Max Luchford
Georgia McKoy
Sasha Macpherson
Adil Majeed
Ned Mansfield
George Markwell
Thomas Mathew
India Megan
Matthew Merrett
Oliver Misick
Shintaro Miyazaki
Sergey Mkhitaryan
Sultaan Mufid
Emily Nearn
Lucy Ockendon
Michael Ogilvy Watson
Jake Parker
Emil Pevtsov
Harry Purnell
Joe Quinn
Ivan Radasinovic
Adib Rasheed
Molly Richardson
Holly Robertson
Freddie Rouse
Paddy Samengo-Turner
Chloe Seale
Abba Shagari
Farzad Shams
Zoe Shaw
Seph Sheehan
Ali Silver
James Singer
Emma Slade
Andrew Sterling
James Studman
Nevada Summerley
Matthew Tee
Sebastian Thomas
Sarah Tong
Dominic Tripp
Celeste Vey
Cluny Wallace
Marco Wan
Michael Welsh

Marie-Pierre Wills
Ali Wilson-Goldsmith
Ben Wood
Vladimir Woodham-Smith
Stefan Zigic

YEAR 8

Bilal Ahmad
Sohrab Ahmed
Ryan Aidat-Sarran
Florence Allen
Miranda Alsina-Olaizola
Hamza Aziz
Niclas Baker
Joss Bates
Barney Beckman
Chloe Bell
Jack Berends
Abdurrahman Bobat
Alex Boitier
Francisco Botelho
Star Brewer
Sebastian Buck
Joey Christian
Theo Christy
Kieran Ciniewicz
Cormac Connelly-Smith
Elliot Cross
Nicholas Cue
Guy Davies
Mahlon Deans
Luka Dinic
Ellie Djukic
Leo Docherty White
Mikey Dorrington Ward
Cameron Edgar
Yan Edwards
Matthew Elliott
Muhammad Essack
Matthew Farmer
Lottie Farrimond
Ryan Flannery
Simon Foreshew
Mimi Forrest
Louis Fox
Alexander Freeland
Howard Goodwin
Oliver Goodwin
Caroline Haddock
Isobel Hamilton
Edward Harwood-Scorer
Max Hawkins
Joseph Hayes
Alex Headley
James Heaney
Francesca Heser
Thomas Hewitt
Sophie Hoare
Guy Horseman
Tobechukwu Ikezue-Clifford

Molly Irwin Clark
Francesca Ivaldi
Taleen Jabbau
Aidan James
Louis Keen
Adnan Khan
Hugo Knox
Sam Lampier
Mahadd Latif
Aleksi Leal-John
Ben Levinson
Perry Lynden
Carmen McClean-Daoust
Isabel Mathie
Gawain Moody
Henry Muscatt
Karin Muya
Imogen Ong
Milan Patel
Eleanor Philcox
Elodie Philip
Stephen Pike
Luke Poysden
Ralph Pritchard
Alice Richardson
Ellie Rose
William Serocold
Rose Sharkey
Zach Shaughnessy Symons
Rory Shaw
Peter Simmonds
Jamie Stapley
Antonis Stylianou
Samuel Swidzinski
Patrick Symes
Holly Tongeman
Martin Turel
Madeleine Vey
Molly Viner
Jake Vithana
Gina Vuqitrna
Sammy Watts Stanfield
Thomas Watts
Megan Williams
Freddie Wills
Gemma Wisdom
Matthew Woolley
Ana Zigic

YEAR 7

Matthew Aikens
Caitlin Airlie
Marcio Andrade
Tom Bailey
Harriet Bain
James Barnes
Lottie Barrett
Minnie Bates
Isabella Berni
Max Berry

William Black
Lunara Bramley-Fenton
Charlie Brown
Jemima Browne
Willa Burton
David Bush
Louis Caro
Amalie Charlesworth
Chetan Chauhan-Sims
Imran Choudhury
Will Clarke
Sabine Coates
Hannah Cox
Michael Crean
Ella Cruz-Cahn
Thomas Davies
Jamie Davis
Mikaela Davis
Sebastian Davis
Ewan Day-Collins
Charlotte Deery
Blue Doughty-White
Tilly Edgcumbe
George Fahmy
Poppy Fitzpatrick
Hamish Frew
Alex Fuller
James Gallagher
Jack Gibbon
Issey Giltrow
William Grice
Alfie Habershon
Jamie Haywood
William Hodsoll
Alexander Hosking
Sameer Hossain
Coco Hoyle-Ansett
Tiger Hutchence
Michael Johnson
Tamara Jovicevic
Jobey Keene
Bella Kemp
Joseph Kenny
Adam Khan
Sam King
Sebastian Krause
Sam Lamiri
Leopold Lansing
Eddie Luchford
Thomas McCahon
Thomas McLoughlin
Ellie Malpas
Harry Mann
Alistair Martin
Jake Martin
Sarah Mathew
Rafi Mauro Benady
Gabriella Mayhew
Kalu Mba
Hattie Miller
Iona Mitchell

Lily Miyazaki
Eleanor Moran
Jack Munkonge
Alex Naudi
Toby Nelson
Wesley Newby
Aurelius Noble
Barney Pierce Jones
Livi Pinkess
Frankie Postles
Lucy Pugh
Harry Robinson
Jamie Rowson
Rosie Rundle
Jamie Ryan
Nadia Saward
Jack Schofield
Freddie Scott-Soundy
Ida Shakespeare
Christopher Shaw
Jasper Stanley
Sasha Sutcliffe
Evie Thomas
Sophie Thompson
Eddie Tyler
Aleksandra Vukojicic
Kimberley Watson
Theo White
Isa Whiteway
Alys Willcox
Pip Williams
Danielle Winder
Maude Wolstenholme

YEAR 6

Maisie Bates
Joe Blewitt
Harry Crocker
Harry Dean
Eddie Green
Solly Heeler
Katja Keane
Felix Lindsell
Michael Milinovich
Olivia Palengat
Joanna Pike
George Russell
Rebecka Salmon
James Setna
Christopher Sharp
Poppy Williams

Emanuel School Boat Club

Great Britain representation since 1967

O = Olympic; W = World; Ltw = Lightweight; EC = European; J = Junior; CDJ = Coupe de la Jeunesse; U23 = Under 23 Match; WSG = World Student Games.

This list does not include the names of those who have rowed for England, Scotland, Wales or Northern Ireland in the Home Championships or those who have rowed in the Oxford and Cambridge Boat Races since 1967. The records for 1966 and earlier can be seen in the School Archives. 1966 was the year when the Emanuel first VIII won the Princess Elizabeth Cup at the Henley Royal Regatta in a record time

NAME	YEAR	EVENT	BOAT	RESULT
G Belchem	1987	CDJ	2SC	2ND
	1988	J	8	-
	1990	U23	4-	3RD
	1992	U23	4-	3RD
P Berners-Lee	1982	LTW	8	6TH
D R Clother	1988	CDJ	2x	-
	1989	J	4+	-
	1990	J	4SC	7TH
S D H Cox	1987	CDJ	2x	2ND
	1988	CDJ	4-	1ST
	1991	U23	4-	2ND
	1992	U23	4-	3RD
	1993	WSG	4-	2ND
	1994	LTW	8	1ST
P Cox	1989	J	2+	-
	1992	LTW	8	2ND
	1993	WSG	8	1ST
R B Crane	1967	J	SC	8TH
N P Dale	1970	J	2SC	9TH
	1978	W	8	7TH
J R Dann	1991	U23	4+	4TH
A M Davidson	1987	J	8	-
	1988	J	8	-
L T O Dillon	2006	CDJ	8	2ND
R A Downie	1975	J	8	9TH
	1978	LTW	8	1ST
	1980	LTW	8	1ST
	1981	LTW	8	-
	1982	LTW	4-	9TH
C M Drury	1970	J	2SC	9TH
	1974	LTW	4-	7TH
	1975	LTW	4-	2ND
	1976	LTW	8	2ND
	1977	LTW	8	1ST
	1978	LTW	8	1ST
	1979	LTW	8	2ND
	1981	LTW	8	-
	1982	LTW	8	5TH
A C Edwards	1994	J	4-	9TH
T Ellis	1989	CDJ	8	1ST

NAME	YEAR	EVENT	BOAT	RESULT
A J French	1975	J	8	9th
	1978	LTW	8	1st
J Z Habba	1994	CDJ	2-	1st
G D Jones	1988	CDJ	4-	1st
	1991	U23	4+	4th
S H Lambert	1975	J	8	9th
A Leighton-Crawford	2006	W	4Sc	4th
	2007	W	Sc	7th
	2007	EC	2Sc	7th
G Lemmens	1975	J	8	9th
M D Field	1975	J	8	9th
M McGowan	1978	W	8	7th
	1980	O	8	2nd
	1981	W	8	2nd
	1984	O	8	6th
A M Obholzer	1986	J	8	-
	1987	U23	4Sc	-
	1988	O	8	4th
	1990	W	8	3rd
V Pardhy	1967	J	2Sc	7th
	1968	J	Sc	3rd
C G Roberts	1975	J	8	9th
	1978	LTW	8	1st
	1980	LTW	8	1st
	1981	LTW	8	-
	1982	W	8	9th
	1984	O	8	6th
G J G Roberts	1975	J	8	9th
N G Roberts	1975	J	8	9th
S P Skeates	1990	CDJ	4+	4th
D A Skinner	1980	J	8	4th
	1984	U23	4+	-
N D C Tee	1967	J	2Sc	7th
	1974	LTW	4-	7th
	1975	LTW	4-	2nd
G Upton	1975	J	8	9th
C Van Besouw	2007	CDJ	4	3rd
H W Waddingham	1988	CDJ	4-	1st
	1989	CDJ	8	1st
R M Waller	1991	J	8	4th
R Wikramaratna	1978	LTW	4-	5th
J A Williams	1990	CDJ	2-	2nd
	1991	J	8	4TH

Careers of selected OEs after leaving Emanuel

The aim of this section is to give a flavour of the ways in which OEs have earned their living after leaving the alma mater. This list is not exhaustive and there are many other OEs not listed here who have distinguished themselves in various walks of life and have brought great credit to themselves as well as to the school.

CREATIVE, MEDIA AND ENTERTAINMENT

NAVEEN ANDREWS – ACTOR. Film and TV credits include: *The Buddha of Suburbia*, *The English Patient* and *Lost*.

MICHAEL ASPEL – TELEVISION PRESENTER. TV credits include *Ask Aspel* and *The Antiques Roadshow*. Awarded the OBE in 1993.

RUPERT DEGAS – ACTOR. West End credits include *Stones in his Pockets* and *The Thirty-nine Steps*.

LESLIE HENSON – ACTOR. Film credits include *Wanted: A Widow*, *Broken Bottles*, *A Warm Corner* and *It's a Boy*. West End credits include *Kissing Time* and *Tons of Money*.

DOUGLAS HICKOX – DIRECTOR. Film credits include *Brannigan*, *Skyriders*, *Entertaining Mr Sloane*, *Theatre of Blood* and *Zulu Dawn*.

CHRIS HUGHES – MUSICIAN. Drummer with the band 'Adam and the Ants'.

KEVIN JACKSON – WRITER AND FILM CRITIC. He was author of *Letters of Introduction: an A–Z of Cultural Heroes and Legends*.

RICHARD MARQUAND – FILM DIRECTOR. Director of *Star Wars: Return of the Jedi* and *Jagged Edge* – two major Hollywood blockbusters.

ANDI PETERS – TV PRESENTER AND PRODUCER. TV credits include *Live and Kicking*, *Children in Need*, *Dancing on Ice*. Producer credits include *An Audience with the Spice Girls*. Currently Executive Editor of Popular Music for the BBC.

MICK ROCK – MUSIC PHOTOGRAPHER. 'The man who shot the 70s': Mick was responsible for many of the iconic album covers from that period including album covers for David Bowie.

He was also associate arts editor of *The Independent*.

MICHEL ROUX – CHEF. Son of Albert Roux, Michel has worked at the three-Michelin-starred Waterside Inn and is currently Head Chef and owner of *Le Gavroche* in Mayfair.

DISTINGUISHED ACADEMICS

PROFESSOR TIM BERNERS-LEE – PHYSICIST AND IT. Widely credited as the creator of the World Wide Web, Sir Tim designed URL and HTTP while working at CERN. He was knighted in 2004. He is a Fellow of the Royal Society. His many awards and accolades include being named as the 'Greatest Briton 2004' and as 'one of the ten most influential people of the 20th century' and being awarded the Order of Merit by Her Majesty the Queen. He is currently working at MIT.

PROFESSOR DEREK FRAY – CHEMIST. Professor of Materials Chemistry at Cambridge since 1996, and Head of the Department of Materials Science and Metallurgy since 2001, Derek Fray is also a Fellow of Fitzwilliam College, Cambridge.

PROFESSOR PETER GODDARD – MATHEMATICAL PHYSICIST. Master of St John's College, Cambridge, from 1994 to 2004. Currently Director of the Institute for Advanced Study at Princeton University. Peter Goddard is a Fellow of the Royal Society and was awarded the CBE in 2002. The painting is by Tom Phillips.

PROFESSOR TONY JUDT – HISTORIAN. His many publications include *Postwar: A History of Europe Since 1945*. Nominated for the 2006 Pulitzer Prize for General Non-Fiction.

Currently Director of the Erich Maria Remarque Institute, NYU.

PROFESSOR DAVID MARQUAND – HISTORIAN. Principal of Mansfield College, Oxford from 1996 to 2002. Labour Party MP and later a founder member of the SDP. Author of many books and numerous articles for the national newspapers.

PROFESSOR DENIS NOBLE – BIOLOGIST. Professor of Cardiovascular Physiology at Oxford University. Fellow of Balliol College. Fellow of the Royal Society. Awarded the CBE in 1998. Author of many books and papers.

PROFESSOR OWEN SAUNDERS – MECHANICAL ENGINEER. Sir Owen was Emeritus Professor of Mechanical Engineering at Imperial College. Earlier in his career Sir Owen was Rector of Imperial College and also Vice-Chancellor of the University of London.

BUSINESS AND INDUSTRY

NEIL CARSON – BUSINESSMAN. Currently Chief Executive of Johnson Matthey plc, a company working with materials technology, employing around 8,000 people in 30 countries.

SIR JOHN PAGE – INDUSTRIALIST. Pursued a career in the oil business following the RAF. Became chairman of the

National Ports Council in1977 until 1980. Was knighted in 1979. He was chairman of the Christie Hospital NHS trust 1991–92.

SIR RONALD WATES – INDUSTRIALIST AND PHILANTHROPIST. Chairman of Wates plc (construction). He set up The Wates Foundation, which gives substantial funding every year to areas of deprivation in the community.

LITERATURE AND JOURNALISM

SIMON BARNES – JOURNALIST. Chief sports correspondent of *The Times*, novelist and amateur bird-watching writer.

STEVE GOOCH – DRAMATIST. Has written over 40 plays including *Female Transport* which premiered at the Royal Shakespeare Company.

N F SIMPSON – DRAMATIST. Plays include *The Hole, One Way Pendulum* and *A Resounding Tinkle*. His plays have been performed at the National Theatre, the Donmar Warehouse and the Royal Court, amongst others.

CLIVE WILMER – POET AND LITERARY CRITIC. Author of many volumes of poetry including *Mystery of Things* and *Devotions*. He also teaches English at Cambridge University.

POLITICS AND PUBLIC SERVICE

SIR ARTHUR GALSWORTHY – DIPLOMAT. British High Commissioner to New Zealand (1969–73) and British Ambassador to Ireland (1973–6).

SIR JOHN GALSWORTHY – DIPLOMAT. British Ambassador to Mexico (1972–77).

THE RT HON. PETER HAIN MP – POLITICIAN. Peter Hain has held several high-profile roles in the Cabinet including Northern Ireland Secretary, Welsh Secretary and Leader of the House of Commons. Has been Labour MP for Neath since 1991.

GEOFFREY ROBINSON MP – POLITICIAN. MP for Coventry North West. Career in the car industry before politics and became Chief Executive of Jaguar cars. He was HM Paymaster General in 1997.

ROYALTY

HIS ROYAL HIGHNESS PRINCE ABDUL-HAKEEM (Wellington 1986–1990) son of Prince Jefri

of Brunei (nephew to the Sultan). Prince Abdul-Hakeem has been a generous benefactor to the school giving £350,000 to building the sixth form centre.

SPORT

The following is just a small sample of the many OEs who have represented their country at international level over the years.

CHRISSIE VAN BESOUW – ROWING. First Emanuel girl to achieve international honours in rowing (she won two bronze medals at the Coupe de la Jeunesse in 2007 while still at school). Leaver in summer 2008.

TONY BODDY – RUGBY. Part of the England squad which toured South Africa in 1971. Currently the manager of the Worcester Warriors.

ISSEY CANNON – CRICKET. Member of the England Women Cricket under 21 squad in summer 2006 while still at school. Leaver in summer 2007.

LUKE DILLON – ROWING. Silver medallist at the Coupe de la Jeunesse in 2006, whilst still at school, rowing for Great Britain in an eight. Leaver in summer 2007.

ALEX LEIGHTON-CRAWFORD – ROWING. Fourth in a lightweight quadruple scull in the 2006 World Championships, seventh in a lightweight single scull in the 2007 World Championships and seventh in a lightweight double scull in the 2007 European Championships.

M MCGOWAN – ROWING. Seventh in the GB eight in the 1978 World Championships, Silver medalist in the GB eight in the 1980 Olympics, Silver medalist in the GB eight in the 1981 World Championships, ninth in the GB eight in the 1982 World Championships, fifth in the GB eight in the 1984 Olympics.

ANTON OBHOLZER – ROWING. Fourth in the Olympics in the Great Britain eight in 1988, fourth in the coxed four at the World Championships in 1990 and third in the GB eight in the World Championships 1991.

BRUCE NEALE – RUGBY. Won three England international

caps in the 1951 Five Nations tournament.

TOM SMITH – RUGBY. Played for Scotland 61 times between 1997 and 2005. He was the only player to play in all six British Lions tests in South Africa and Australia in 1997 and 2001.

STUART SURRIDGE – CRICKET. Player, captain and finally president of Surrey County Cricket Club. One of three Old Emanuel pupils to hold the Presidency (the others are Vic Dodds and Derek Newman).

JENNA WALTERS – GYMNASTICS. Jenna represented England in matches against South Africa and Russia in October 2007 while still at school. Leaver in summer 2008.

Index

Illustrations are entered in *italics*